The Ecology and Management of Prairies in the Central United States

PUBLISHED FOR THE NATURE CONSERVANCY BY THE UNIVERSITY OF IOWA PRESS, IOWA CITY

the ecology and management of prairies in the central united states

CHRIS HELZER *with photos by the author*

A Bur Oak Book

University of Iowa Press, Iowa City 52242
Copyright © 2010 by The Nature Conservancy
www.uiowapress.org
Printed in Canada

Design by Kristina Kachele Design, llc

The University of Iowa Press is a member of Green Press Initiative and is committed to preserving natural resources.

Printed on acid-free paper
Library of Congress Cataloging-in-Publication Data
Helzer, Chris, 1972–
The ecology and management of prairies in the central United States / by Chris Helzer; with photos by the author.
    p.   cm.—(A Bur oak book)
Includes bibliographical references and index.
ISBN-13: 978-1-58729-865-3 (pbk.)
ISBN-10: 1-58729-865-1 (pbk.)
1. Prairie ecology—Middle West. 2. Prairies—Middle West—Management. I. Title.
QH104.5.M47H45 2010
577.4'40978—dc22   2009035059

contents

appendices

Preface

My primary purpose for writing this book was to educate prairie owners and managers about grassland ecology and to provide them with guidance on making sound decisions about managing their prairies. This book does not offer a recipe for creating pretty prairies or abundant wildlife. Instead, I present background information about how prairies work and ideas for how to mix and match management techniques in ways that will keep prairies vigorous and viable.

The goal of prairie management, as presented here, is to sustain diverse communities of plants and animals. That diversity is important not only for the sake of the species themselves but also because diverse communities are more resilient in the face of a multitude of serious threats to prairies, including habitat fragmentation, invasive species, and climate change.

This book is intended principally for landowners with a strong interest in understanding and nurturing their prairie but without a strong background in ecology or land management. However, it should also be useful to people who don't own or manage their own prairies but who have a strong interest in them. The information is certainly applicable to farming and ranching, but this is not a book on how to make a living from grasslands. My suggested management techniques will not prevent prairies from being profitable, but I did not design them for that specific purpose.

Grasslands can be found throughout much of North America, and the ideas and strategies in this book should apply to most of them. However, the book is particularly aimed at tallgrass and mixed-grass prairies in the central part of North America (see figure 1). Most of my experience with hands-on prairie management comes from the western portion of that range, so the book may have a slight western bias. However, I have also spent a great deal of time working with prairie managers and ecologists from the eastern edges of tall-grass prairie, and I have worked to ensure that this book incorporates their ideas and experiences as well. I sent the manuscript to a dozen biologists and land managers from across the region to make sure that there were no factual errors in the background information or serious objections to proposed management strategies. Some of the information in this book will become out of date over time as prairie managers develop new ideas and techniques. Updates on prairie management techniques can be found on the website PrairieNebraska.org.

It is necessary that I define several terms that are used throughout this book. First, unless otherwise stated, the term "prairie" simply means a grassland that has a diverse plant community dominated by native grasses and wildflowers. Prairies that have survived the last couple hundred years without being plowed under for rowcrop farming are called remnant prairies. Prairies that have been reseeded on land formerly farmed or otherwise severely altered are called restored prairies. Both remnant and restored prairies fall within the definition of prairie in this book because they require thoughtful management in order to maintain their biological diversity.

In spite of a wealth of experience among a number of very smart prairie ecologists, surprisingly little information on prairie management is widely available. In this book I've tried to remedy that by synthesizing what I've learned from others and from my own experience. It's not the last word on how to manage prairies, but I hope it captures the most important concepts as we understand them today.

Acknowledgments

I've been incredibly fortunate to be able to spend the last fifteen years exploring, studying, and managing prairies. My job with The Nature Conservancy has taken me to grasslands across North America and allowed me to participate in a large network of people who are entranced by and devoted to prairies. This book was made possible by many persons who have mentored me and by lots of colleagues who have intelligently traded ideas back and forth over the years. I am particularly grateful to Steve Winter for introducing me to prairies, Bill Whitney for making me look more closely at them, Al Steuter for helping me understand them, and Brent Lathrop for letting me try out crazy management ideas. Thank you to Gerry Steinauer for being a great friend and fellow ecologist and for graciously saving me from many tedious hours buried in a plant key. I am also deeply indebted to Jon Farrar and Mike Forsberg for their honest criticism and support of my photography.

Ron and Judy Parks generously provided funding for the color photography throughout this book, which wouldn't have been nearly the same without their contribution. I am deeply grateful.

The following people kindly reviewed all or some of this book; I very much appreciate their time and input: Gerry Steinauer, Gen Helzer, Mardell Jasnowski, Chris Rundstrom, Clay Nielsen, Jill Wells, Bob Hamilton, Craig

Allen, Ellen Jacquart, Joel Jorgensen, John Shuey, Scott Taylor, Steve Clubine, Jarren Kuipers, Ron and Judy Parks, Gary and Lori Schneekloth, and Marva Weigelt.

Finally, thank you to my wife, Gen, for her love, support, patience, and editing.

Introduction

Prairies are incredibly complex and diverse natural communities. They evolved under harsh conditions: huge herds of bison, expansive fires, and extended droughts. In many places they've now been largely replaced by row-crop agriculture and urban sprawl or degraded by years of continuous severe grazing, haphazard herbicide use, tree invasion, and the introduction of non-native grasses and wildflowers. Those that remain are often relegated to steep terrain or to places where rocks or moisture make farming difficult.

Because of their scarcity, it's critically important that the remaining prairies retain as much biological diversity as possible. Prairies thrive when they're subjected to periodic intense disturbances like fire and grazing. They stagnate and lose their integrity when those disturbances are withheld. Invasive species can quickly degrade the plant diversity and habitat quality of a prairie if they are allowed to gain a foothold. The risk of invasion is compounded in fragmented landscapes where prairies are smaller and more exposed to the sources of those invaders. Because of all these factors, thoughtful management is essential to the continued health and survival of prairie communities.

This book is an attempt to provide background and guidance to prairie managers trying to preserve the biological diversity of native grasslands. It is split into two major sections. The first section is an overview of the complex workings of prairies. Within that section, chapter 1 describes plants and the communities they live in, and chapter 2 details the way in which those plant

Tallgrass prairie like the Greene Prairie Restoration at the University of Wisconsin–Madison Arboretum can harbor diverse populations of both plants and animals.

communities are modified and regulated by natural and human-induced disturbances. Chapter 3 discusses prairie animals. Chapters 4 and 5 illustrate the importance of diversity within plant and animal communities and the landscape context within which natural processes operate. The second section builds upon the ecological information from the first section and provides guidance for developing effective management strategies. Specifically, chapters 6 and 7 describe the general process of adaptive management and the guiding principles for designing appropriate management strategies. Chapter 8 illustrates various management systems that can help achieve certain objectives. Chapters 9 and 10 lay out guidance for dealing with species that have particular habitat requirements and for invasive species. Chapter 11 includes general information related to prairie restoration techniques. Following a short conclusion, the "Note on Climate Change" discusses the role and importance of prairie management in the context of a rapidly changing climate. Eight appendices are also included to provide more specific information on management tools as well as other sources of information related to the topics in this book. The first three appendices provide more detail on grazing, prescribed fire, and invasive species, respectively. The

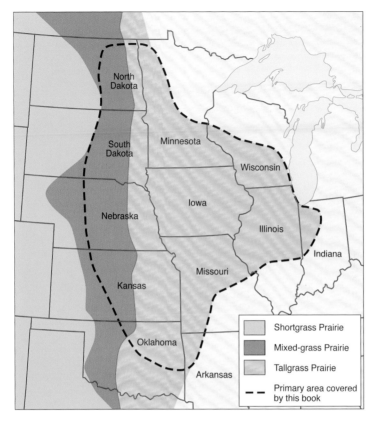

Figure 1. The information presented in this book is intended to apply to the majority of North America's tallgrass and mixed-grass prairie regions.

fourth provides a contact list for local expertise in your state and is followed by bibliographic information and sources of additional reading.

Most of the information in this book and its general management philosophies should apply to grasslands anywhere in North America. However, the specific management strategies and recommendations are most relevant to prairies in the following areas: eastern North Dakota, eastern South Dakota, eastern Nebraska, eastern Kansas, eastern Oklahoma, northwestern Missouri, northern Illinois, northwestern Indiana, Iowa, southwestern Wisconsin, and southwestern Minnesota (figure 1).

prairie ecology

The Griffith Prairie, owned and managed by Prairie Plains Resources Institute, is a mixed-grass prairie in Nebraska. Mixed-grass prairies have plant species characteristic of both tallgrass and shortgrass prairies, and their species composition and habitat structure can vary greatly from year to year depending upon rainfall and management.

So what is a prairie? Prairies are diverse ecological communities in which grasses are the dominant plants. The lack of trees is the criterion most used to discriminate between prairies and other ecological communities. Trees and shrubs are often present in and around prairies, but if there are more than a few widely scattered trees the community is classified as a savanna or even a woodland. However, there is also a difference between prairies and other kinds of grasslands. Prairies contain a diverse mixture of native plant species, including grasses, sedges, and wildflowers. Grasslands that are dominated by only a few plant species, especially nonnative grasses, lack the ability to support the majority of prairie-dependent species, and thus are not considered to be prairies.

Prairies are often split into three types: tallgrass, mixed-grass, and shortgrass. There are no hard lines defining the boundaries between these types. Instead, prairies tend to become gradually shorter in western regions of the Great Plains because of lower rainfall. This book is most relevant to tallgrass and mixed-grass prairies.

Historically, prairies were created and maintained by three interconnected natural processes: climate, fire, and grazing. Fire and climate interact to help prevent trees from becoming overabundant. Fire and grazing interact to create and maintain a diverse plant community that supports a myriad of other prairie species. When those processes are eliminated, most prairies transform into low-diversity grasslands or even woodlands.

Prairies can also be destroyed by conversion to rowcrop agriculture or other human developments or by broadcast herbicide applications or similar activities that kill the majority of prairie species. Conservative estimates put the loss of tallgrass prairie at about 96 percent. The loss of mixed-grass prairie is not quite as severe but is still around 75 percent in many states.

Although many prairies have been unable to survive the spread of industrial agriculture and the intensive human development of the Great Plains, prairies do have the ability to thrive under many other difficult conditions. Since the end of the last ice age, North American prairies have survived in a landscape where the climate can vary wildly from wet to dry and hot to cold. Large fires, typically followed by intensive grazing, were regular occurrences over the last 5,000 to 12,000 years. As a result, prairies are inhabited by a wide variety of plant and animal species that have the adaptability to survive those events.

The incredible diversity of life in a prairie also means that every decision that relates to the management of a prairie will have an impact on a vast number of species, including plants, animals, insects, and tiny microorganisms. A good prairie manager needs to be well informed in order to make decisions that will help protect the long-term diversity and resilience of the prairie. The first section of this book is intended to be a primer on what prairies are and how they work.

A plant community includes all of the plants that grow and interact together in a particular place. Each member of a plant community has a unique survival strategy that shapes the way it interacts with its neighbors. The diversity of those strategies strengthens the community as a whole because it increases the community's ability to respond to drought, flooding, intense grazing, fire, and other kinds of disturbances.

A high-quality prairie can have as many as 150 to 300 species of plants. As a grassland manager, you'll find it useful to be familiar with all or most of those plants, so you can evaluate their responses to your management. But for most people it's not reasonable to become familiar with 300 species of plants, and even experienced biologists don't know the individual growth and reproductive needs of that many species. So although every plant species has unique characteristics, we can split them into groups with somewhat similar life strategies. This allows us to devise effective management plans and track the way the plant community reacts to those plans as they're carried out.

This book isn't designed to teach you how to identify plant species, but there are a number of excellent field guides that can help with that. Your best bet is to find the most locally produced guide available because that will limit the number of possible species to sort through. Wildflower guides that cover half of North America, for example, are usually so general that they are of

Manystem pea often colonizes steep slopes in loess prairies. Topography has a strong influence on the makeup of plant communities.

little use. The Internet is an excellent source of information on plants. Several suggestions for field guides and other resources are listed in appendix 7.

Grouping Plants by Type

The most obvious way to divide plants is to split them into grasses, forbs, and woody plants. Grasses are the first kind of plant most people think of when picturing a prairie, and they make up the highest percentage of prairie biomass. There are many species of grass in prairies, ranging in size from very small to very large. It's not unusual for a small prairie to contain more than 20 species of grass. Prairies also contain other plants closely related to grasses, including sedges, rushes, and others that are similar in many respects but have significant differences. For now, we'll lump them together. Sedges and rushes are an important component of lowland prairies, where they can be as diverse and abundant as grasses, but many sedges are also common in upland prairies.

Forbs are flowering plants that are not grasses, trees, or shrubs. They are often called broad-leaved plants but include many that look like grasses until they flower. They include all the showy wildflowers in prairies but also many plants that have much less conspicuous flowers.

Sedges are grasslike plants that stay green for more of the year than do many other prairie plants and often have stems with a triangular cross section. They are common in most prairies but not often recognized for their importance.

Woody plants include both trees and shrubs. One important distinction between woody plants and herbaceous plants (grasses, sedges, and forbs) is that trees and shrubs have their growing points above the ground and most herbaceous plants have their growing points at or below the ground's surface. This means that a tree or shrub starts growing in the spring from near the tip of its aboveground stems. In contrast, most other plants start over at the ground in the spring and grow new stems next to the dead ones from last year.

Grouping Plants by Season

Another helpful way to characterize plants is to divide them into cool-season and warm-season plants (figure 2). Cool-season plants grow best in the kinds of conditions found in the spring and fall but don't do well under very hot conditions. These plants grow strongly and bloom during the spring and early summer and then often go into dormancy, or at least slow their growth dramatically, during the hot part of the summer. In years of good fall moisture, they may grow again for a while at that time of year. Common cool-season

prairie plants include Canada and Virginia wildrye, the native wheatgrasses and fescues, and most sedges and spring wildflowers.

Warm-season plants thrive under warm midsummer conditions and will wait until late spring or even early summer to emerge from the ground. They have their peak growth period and bloom during the summer months and then enter dor-

Big bluestem, a warm-season grass, and Canada wildrye, a cool-season grass, are two major native grasses in prairies.

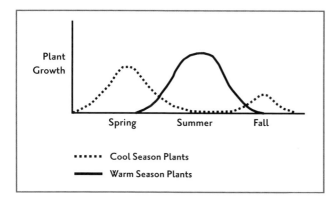

Figure 2. Generalized growth periods of warm-season and cool-season plants.

mancy as temperatures cool off in the fall. Warm-season prairie plants include most of the best-known grasses like big bluestem, Indiangrass, switchgrass, and prairie dropseed, along with many common summer wildflowers.

Grouping Plants by Strategy

A third way to identify plants is as "colonizers" or "occupiers." Colonizers are plants that can take advantage of open spaces quickly. They often live short lives (1–2 years) and produce an enormous number of seeds. Their seeds disperse easily and are good at germinating and growing very quickly, but they need lots of light so they aren't able to get started under other plants that are already well established. Some well-known colonizers are those plants we consider to be weeds because they take advantage of overstressed areas of our yards and pastures. Examples of these include dandelions, oxalis, crabgrass, and prostrate spurge. In prairies, most of the colonizers are native plants, and they play a vital role in maintaining healthy native prairie communities. Because colonizers are short-lived they can serve as indicators that the dominant grasses have weakened, but they typically disappear when those grasses get their strength back. Some common native colonizer plants in prairies include common evening primrose, prairie fleabane, ragweed, and annual sunflowers.

Occupiers are essentially the opposite of colonizers. They often live long lives (up to 40 years or more) and tend not to produce many seeds each time they bloom. In fact, these plants may not bloom at all in years of drought

Rhizomatous plants like this grass avoid many of the risks and uncertainties associated with reproduction by seed. New plants can grow from rhizomes sent out by the parent plant and receive supportive nutrients from that parent while developing their own root systems.

Type	Grass	Grasslike, oval stem
	Sedge	Grasslike, triangular stem
	Rush	Grasslike, round stem
	Forb	Broadleaf, nonwoody stem
	Woody plant	Broadleaf, woody stem
Season	Warm-season	Primary growth in summer
	Cool-season	Primary growth in spring/fall
Strategy	Colonizer	Moves quickly, competes poorly
	Occupier	Moves slowly, competes well

Figure 3. Plant groupings and definitions.

Grasses

	Warm-season	Cool-season
Colonizer	Witchgrass	Sixweeks fescue
Occupier	Big bluestem	Western wheatgrass

Forbs

	Warm-season	Cool-season
Colonizer	Blackeyed Susan	Prairie ragwort
Occupier	Maximilian sunflower	Wild indigo

Figure 4. Examples of plant species in various groups.

or other stresses. Most colonizers must bloom and produce seeds each year regardless of conditions because they will die at the end of the year. In contrast, occupiers have time to spare and often save energy by not blooming in a tough year or even going dormant during really bad times and reemerging when conditions are better. Many occupiers can also reproduce underground, by sending out rhizomes that produce new plants, without having to rely on seeds. Rhizomes act as the lifeline between the parent plant and its offspring, and provide the new plants with energy to help them survive tough competition more easily than isolated seedlings can. Occupiers are not built for speed, so they don't expand quickly into bare ground. But once they become established they can stay there a long time, even under extreme stress. Common occupiers in native prairie include many of the best-known grasses and flowers such as big bluestem, switchgrass, prairie clover, stiff sunflower, and other perennial sunflowers.

Both colonizers and occupiers are critical to prairies. When bare ground opens up or when dominant grasses are weakened by a summer fire or repeated grazing, colonizers move in quickly and establish a presence. That quick establishment helps fill open spaces and stabilize the soil until the slower occupiers can take over again. Once the occupiers are reestablished, the colonizers disappear, but leave millions of seeds behind to take advantage of future disturbances. Because many invasive plant species are also colonizers, it is important to have a healthy population of native colonizers to help outcompete the invasives.

Grouping plants by various categories can help with identification of species, but can also clarify their habitat and survival requirements. It is important to remember, however, that these categories are created by humans and many plant species can exhibit characteristics of more than one category of type, season, or strategy. A summary of categories and some example species of each are presented on the previous page (see figures 3 and 4).

Defining Plant Communities

The composition of plant species in any particular place is determined by a variety of factors. On a broad scale, annual precipitation and other associated climatic conditions separate prairie into tallgrass and shortgrass ecosystems, with mixed-grass prairie in between. But on a more local scale, plant communities can be defined by the combination of topography and soil.

The topography of a site has great influence over the kinds of plants that can persist there. Lowland sites capture more moisture than upland sites, and some are especially wet because they have groundwater near the surface. Those sub-irrigated prairies, or wet meadows, are often dominated by wetland sedges and grasses such as prairie cordgrass. Wet meadows are often located along river floodplains or in deep valleys, and they usually support much taller vegetation than do nearby uplands. Within those meadows, a very small change in altitude can have a tremendous influence on the plant community because it changes the depth to groundwater.

Upland prairies are affected by both the slope and the aspect of their site.

The upland prairie at The Nature Conservancy's Hitchcock Nature Preserve in the Loess Hills of Iowa has a plant community very different from that of a lowland prairie because of both the soils and slopes at the site. In addition, both the steepness and aspect of the slopes determine the species of plants that grow well there.

Plants growing on steeper slopes are less able to capture rainfall before it runs downhill than plants growing on more gradual slopes. South- and west-facing slopes catch more direct sunlight than north- and east-facing slopes, and experience warmer and drier conditions. All of these factors determine the plant species that can survive at a particular site and the height to which those species can grow.

The soil underneath a prairie also plays a large role in determining plant community type. Sandy or gravelly soils allow water to drain through them relatively quickly because the spaces between soil particles are large and do not hold water tightly. A heavier soil, with more clay and loam particles, does not permit water to move through it as quickly, and smaller pore spaces hold on to water more tightly. In addition, the amount of organic matter in the soil influences the ability of the soil to hold moisture and to provide nutrients to plants. Plants growing in sandy soils with low organic matter have to be better adapted to variable moisture conditions than do those in richer soils. Of course, plant communities also influence the soil beneath them. Tallgrass prairie produces much more vegetative material each year than shortgrass prairie, and when those plants decay, the soil beneath accumulates much thicker layers of organic matter. The higher amount of organic matter then provides moisture and nutrients and allows plants to grow larger, creating a feedback loop.

The organic matter of a prairie also helps maintain communities of soil organisms, including bacteria and fungi. Among other roles, these tiny organisms help to drive decomposition of vegetation and to convert nutrients into forms more available for plants. Mycorrhizal fungi, for example, are well known for their ability to fix soil nitrogen (making it accessible for uptake by plants). In fact, some prairie restoration efforts may be hampered by the absence or scarcity of these fungi in soils, making it difficult to establish some kinds of plants, particularly legumes. While the research on soil microorganisms has increased in recent years, we still know very little about the complexity and importance of this group of species and the way in which it affects plant communities.

To summarize, prairie plant communities are extremely complex. It's not necessary to understand all of the inner workings of plant communities, but it is important to understand some of the common characteristics of plants within various groups, and how those plants interact with each other and with their environment. Recognizing which plants grow under certain kinds of conditions can help you assess whether those conditions are changing, and whether you need to adjust your management accordingly. The next chapter will expand on the conditions prairie plants have to adapt to, including the kinds of stresses that plants endure in prairies, and how plants and plant communities respond to those stresses.

2. The Role of Disturbance

Since the final retreat of the glaciers, grasslands have dominated most of what is now the central United States. During that time they have survived frequent fires, intensive grazing by native herbivores, and extreme climatic conditions. In fact, those "disturbances" shaped prairies, helped maintain their character, and made them diverse and resilient.

One of the most important roles of disturbance in grasslands is to shift the competitive advantage within the plant community. Under a static set of conditions (no fire, grazing, or drought), certain plant species would be best suited to those conditions and thrive. Species not as well adapted would lose vigor, suffer reduced reproductive ability, and eventually be pushed out of the prairie altogether. In order for a plant to remain in a prairie, it needs favorable conditions to occur often enough for it to survive and replace itself in the system. Disturbances such as fire, grazing, and drought can each suppress certain kinds of dominant plants, allowing other plants to thrive.

Fire

Fire is a critical component of the ecology of grasslands. Fires were and are started by lightning strikes, but Native American people were historically responsible for igniting fires as well. Because people have been active in central North American prairies for as long as those prairies have existed, it's impossible to separate the two. Native Americans used fire for everything from attracting game to warfare. Scientists have attempted to determine the average frequency of fires in prairies by looking at the burn scars on old trees. In general, they have found that the average parcel of tallgrass prairie was burned about once every 3–4 years, while mixed-grass prairie burned slightly less frequently (once every 5–8 years). However, those are rough averages, and the frequency varied widely over time. There has been much speculation about the historical timing of fires. It is often suggested that most lightning fires took place during the late summer when most dry lightning strikes occur. These probably covered relatively little area because fires burned slowly in the green vegetation. On the other hand, the dry grass that fuels fires is most flammable during the late fall and early spring, so the largest fires may have occurred at those times.

Regardless of the historical frequency or season of fires, they certainly played a critical part in shaping the structure and function of prairies. One of the most important roles of fire is that of keeping trees and shrubs at bay. Some trees, such as eastern redcedars, are extremely vulnerable to fire and are killed by any fire that scorches their stems and needles. Most deciduous trees, on the other hand, are not usually killed by fire, but can be weakened considerably—especially if they are burned during the growing season. If those deciduous trees are small and their trunks are unprotected by thick bark, a hot fire will cook the stems sufficiently to kill all the living tissue above the ground. In that case, the tree has to start over from the roots, which both weakens it and makes it more vulnerable to browsing animals like deer, elk, and rabbits. Larger trees with thick layers of bark, like bur oaks, often survive the initial heat of the fire, although very hot fires can sometimes heat less-protected stems higher in a tree enough to severely stress or even kill it. Repeated fires can affect even large, well-established trees by burning away enough bark to expose them to insects or diseases that can eventually kill them.

In places like Iowa and Missouri, the front lines of the battle between open prairie and deciduous woodlands were marked by prairie savannas—scattered large trees with grass surrounding them. In periods of wetter climate, trees probably pushed out into the prairies, but drier periods had more frequent fires and pushed the trees back again. In the western prairies, trees were found mainly along streams, ridges, or ravines where fires were infrequent or less intense.

In addition to their effect on trees, historical fires contributed to the diversity and function of prairies in many other ways. Because most prairie plants die back to the ground each fall, they leave their dead stems and leaves on the surface. Those stems and leaves fall over and can form a dense thatch over the years. That thatch, or litter, slows the warming of the soil in the spring and delays the beginning of the growing season. It can also shade out many smaller plants and restrict the growth of larger plants. However, that accumulation of thatch also increases the vulnerability of prairie to fire. When a fire burns through, it removes thatch and exposes bare soil again, allowing both established plants and new seedlings full sunlight to grow. In addition, some plant species have higher seed germination rates following a fire because the smoke and/or the heat of the fire actually help the seed to germinate.

The season during which a fire occurs has a lot to do with its impact on the plant community. Fires during the dormant season (late fall through early spring) burn when most of the vegetation is dormant, so there is very little negative impact on most plants, and they can take advantage of the bare soil conditions when the growing season begins. Cool-season plants benefit the most from dormant-season fires because they are the first to emerge in the spring.

Dormant-season fires can set woody plants back by making them start over at ground level. However, some species, such as smooth sumac, respond to that stress by suckering out and forming multiple new shoots where only one existed before. With that strategy, sumac can actually form a thicker patch following a dormant-season fire than it had before. Eventually, if browsing animals don't control them, those patches can become dense enough that no grass grows underneath them, making them nearly invulnerable to future fires.

Fires that occur during the growing season have much different impacts. Growing-season fires are usually slower moving and less likely to burn large areas than dormant-season fires. The fires are fueled by the dried grass from previous seasons, but the combination of higher humidities and abundant

green vegetation causes slow-moving and very smoky fires. However, because prairie vegetation is actively growing when these fires move through, the impact on vegetation can be significant. The plants growing most strongly at the time of the fire are most affected. Fires during the late spring or early summer set back cool-season plants and allow warm-season plants to begin their growth period with less competition for light and water. In contrast, fires during the summer suppress the growth of warm-season plants and favor cool-season plants. Summer fires also tend to release many annual and biennial plants (colonizers) because the suppression of the dominant warm-season grasses opens up space for new seedlings to emerge. This often results in an abundance of showy flowers during the fall and through the next growing season. However, it can also facilitate more vigorous growth of invasive cool-season grasses in prairies where they are a concern.

Growing-season fires also have a stronger impact on trees and shrubs than dormant-season fires, because all the energy those woody plants have invested in that year's growth is lost. The most vulnerable time for most trees and shrubs is in the late spring just after they leaf out. Woody plants rely on energy stored in their roots over the winter to produce their first leaves. A fire that comes through just as they finish those leaves and before the leaves have time to produce new energy can severely stress the plant.

In many parts of the Great Plains where prairie survives today, fire is either absent or much less frequent than it was historically. If grazing (or haying) is also absent, the accumulation of thatch can lead to a steep decline in species diversity as smaller plants are excluded and even many taller plants find it difficult to survive. More important, prairies that are excluded from fire are often quickly invaded by trees and shrubs. The encroachment is faster in eastern prairies where the moist climate is more favorable for rapid tree growth, but it occurs in western prairies as well. In the absence of fire, trees and shrubs that would otherwise have been restricted to steep slopes and riparian areas spread quickly. If they are allowed enough time, they can grow large enough to survive fire when it returns. Even if fire periodically sets them back, a sufficient number of good growing seasons between fires will allow those trees and shrubs to continue expanding their root systems, increasing the speed and vigor with which they rebound from fires.

Grassland fires can be dramatic, but prairie plants are well adapted to them and can regrow quickly after the fire has passed.

During a lengthy absence of fire, the spread of trees can increase exponentially. As more trees become established across a landscape, the rain of seed comes harder and from more directions. In many places, trees have become sufficiently established in the landscape surrounding small prairies that even frequent fires cannot stave off the invasion.

Grazing

All prairies have evolved with herbivores (plant-eating animals). While an image of a large herd of grazing bison scattered across the plains may be the first to come to mind for most people, bison were not the only grazers in prairies. Many other animals lived and grazed in historical prairies, including large mammals like deer, elk, and pronghorn, and smaller ones such as prairie dogs, rabbits, voles, and mice. Most of those animals ate a varied diet that included trees, shrubs, forbs, and grasses, along with their seeds. In addition, insects were (and are) extremely important herbivores in prairies. Grasshoppers and other leaf-eating insects consume enormous amounts of vegetation, rivaling the amount eaten by bison in any particular place. In addition to direct grazing, many insects affect plants in other ways, by sucking juices, clipping leaves and flowers, and otherwise disrupting and inhibiting their growth.

While there were many herbivores in historical prairies, the dominant large grazer was the plains bison. Estimates of the numbers of bison that spread across the plains vary widely, but they certainly numbered in the millions and had a profound effect on prairies and prairie plants. Herds changed their location from year to year and throughout each season, which introduced a high degree of variability into the impact they had on the vegetation of any particular place. Bison were known to have moved as far east and south as Florida, but their historical abundance in any particular place is often the subject of much academic discussion and argument.

It's impossible to consider the movement and impact of bison without thinking about fire. From what we know about historical bison behavior, large herds would congregate on recently burned areas of prairie, particularly in the spring and early summer. Native Americans, of course, took advantage of that by using fire to attract and find bison herds each year. As the summer wore on, herds probably split into smaller groups and spread out across larger

Bison at The Nature Conservancy's Niobrara Valley Preserve in the sandhills of Nebraska. While bison are present at several large preserves managed by the Conservancy and other conservation organizations, there are very few places where they can operate on the scale they did historically.

areas. So, grazing by bison in the early part of the season was likely very intense in burned areas, and then less so as the animals scattered later in the summer. Areas of grasslands that were not recently burned probably had little or no bison grazing. The burned areas that were intensively grazed in one year would probably take 1–3 years (depending upon moisture) to recover enough vegetation to support another fire. This created a shifting mosaic of burned, grazed, and recovering patches across huge landscapes.

Today, bison are present on some of the larger grasslands in the mixed-grass and tallgrass prairie regions, particularly on sites owned and managed by The Nature Conservancy and other conservation organizations. In those areas where fire is used to shift and concentrate their grazing on different parts of their pasture each year, bison probably interact with the prairie much as they used to. The study of that behavior has revealed some interesting contrasts between that kind of bison grazing and the way cattle graze the same kinds of pastures.

While both cattle and bison eat grass as the major part of their diet, bison have been shown to eat grass almost exclusively, while cattle eat a more mixed diet of grasses and forbs. Thus, bison grazing probably played a large role in maintaining a diverse plant community in prairies. The intensive grazing following fires would have severely stressed the dominant grasses in those areas and opened up room for new seedlings of any plants able to take advantage of the situation. And if forbs largely avoided being grazed, they would be growing and flowering, relatively untouched, in the midst of those suppressed grasses. This should have allowed those forbs to win back space lost to grasses during periods without grazing, and kept the overall plant diversity in prairies high.

Today, most of the grazing that occurs in prairies is by cattle—and normally done for the purpose of livestock production, not plant community diversity, although good ranchers recognize the value of both. However, in production-oriented grazing systems many forbs (and some grasses) disappear because they are grazed repeatedly over long periods of time and eventually replaced by plant species that are less palatable to cattle. Because bison require large grasslands (5,000 acres or more) to function relatively "naturally," and cattle grazing has been perceived to reduce plant diversity, many prairie managers do not use grazing animals as a tool for prairie management. This has led to the absence of one of the most important processes, or disturbances, that regulate prairie function.

However, there are ways to use cattle grazing in a targeted manner to help increase and maintain diversity in prairie communities. In the last decade, scientists and conservationists have experimented with cattle and fire together in an attempt to replicate some of the positive effects of the bison/fire interaction. This "patch-burn grazing" has shown some very positive results for wildlife habitat and plant diversity. Patch-burn grazing and other grazing systems will be discussed much more in chapter 8.

Climate

The third major disturbance to prairies is climate. About 10,500 years ago, deciduous forest had become the dominant land cover in much of central North America. As the climate became warmer and drier over the next several thousand years, grassland spread from west to east across the plains, replacing the woodland as it went. Since that time, there have been several relatively major climate shifts, but prairies have survived them all.

For the last 4,000 years, the climate has been dominated by relatively cool and wet conditions. However, those years often included long dry periods during the hot summer months and extended (multiple-year) severe droughts that occurred every 30 years or so. The intensity and frequency of severe droughts in the western regions of the prairie, along with less annual rainfall, helps to separate shortgrass prairie from tallgrass prairie.

The eastern extent of the tallgrass prairie is commonly considered to be somewhere around Indianapolis, Indiana. There are certainly pockets of prairie to the east of that point, but if you drew a line from Indianapolis to Tulsa, Oklahoma, and another from Indianapolis to Fargo, North Dakota, you would pretty closely delineate the eastern edge of the main block of tallgrass prairie. Interestingly, recent analysis of current and historical climatic conditions by some Illinois researchers has shown that several important patterns coincide very closely with those lines.

For example, over the last 100 years or so the percentage of drought years in the prairie region was about double that of the wooded areas to the northeast and southeast of the tallgrass prairie. In addition, the timing of precipitation through the year appears to be important. Deciduous forest requires fairly consistent precipitation year-round. In the oak-hickory woodlands to the east and south of the tallgrass prairie, nearly half of the annual precipitation falls in the cold half of the year. But tallgrass prairie receives much less precipitation during that time, and it turns out that those dry winters may be an important factor in keeping deciduous woodland out of the prairie region.

Climate alone cannot keep trees out of prairies, as can be seen by the rapid spread of woody plants into many small grasslands today. But historical climatic conditions greatly influenced fire frequency. Dry weather, punctuated by frequent thunderstorms, helped spawn fires that spread over large

expanses of the relatively flat topography. Frequent large fires helped prevent woody vegetation from invading prairies. While those fires were started by people as well as lightning, there is no doubt that thunderstorm frequency was important. The prairie region is one of three prime areas of thunderstorm activity in the United States, the other two being Florida and the Gulf Coast. Thunderstorms in the tallgrass prairie are 3–6 times more frequent during the fire-prone times of the year than they are in the forests to the north. In addition, the number and frequency of cloud-to-ground lightning strikes are much lower to the north of the prairie/forest border.

Thunderstorms influence prairies in important ways. Much of the summer moisture received by prairies comes from sporadic thunderstorms, which means that rainfall is relatively unpredictable and can vary widely even within small geographic areas. Lightning was also an important source of historical prairie fires.

Invertebrates are small but important members of prairie communities. Herbivorous insects, including this caterpillar, have enormous influence on the growth rates and strategies of plants and also provide food sources for many other prairie animals.

3. Animal Communities

Prairie animals need better public relations agents. A few, like bison and prairie-chickens, are fairly well recognized by the general public, but the majority of prairie animals spend most of their time either underground or hidden in the grass, so seeing them is a rare event. Besides that, the vast majority of prairie animals are invertebrates, which don't typically rank high on popularity charts. However, while knowing plants can help you identify a prairie from other plant communities, and even give you a pretty good idea of prairie quality, if you don't know about prairie invertebrates, you don't really know about prairies.

Invertebrates

Insects are incredibly abundant and important components of the world's ecosystems. At this point, 1.7 million insect species have been described (discovered and distinguished from other species by entomologists). However, there are many more species that have not yet been described, particularly in the tropics. Scientists estimate that there are actually closer to 10 million species of insects, and the number may be as high as 80 million. Worldwide, invertebrates as a group make up more than 80 percent of all species of living things. Vertebrates, by comparison, make up about 0.4 percent. Plants and algae are about 4 percent, and microorganisms are about 15 percent.

In North America alone, there are an estimated 163,000 or so species of insects, and another 35,000 species of arachnids (spiders, mites, ticks, scorpions, etc.) There are more species of flies (37 percent of the total) than any other insect group in North America, followed by the group that includes bees and wasps, and then beetles.

The diversity of insects mirrors the diversity of roles and functions they have in their ecosystems. Insects are major contributors to some of the critical functions in ecosystems and natural communities, including decomposition, nutrient cycling, pollination, soil formation, herbivory, predation, and parasitism. In prairies, many insects and other invertebrates live underground for all or part of their lives, helping to maintain soil structure and nutrient levels and feeding on plants (and each other). In fact, some research estimates that the biomass of belowground invertebrates is 10 times higher than that of those living above ground. Unfortunately, we know relatively little about belowground invertebrates, let alone how they influence prairie ecology or respond to grassland management.

Even aboveground insects still need considerably more study. In fact, it's still fairly common to find new species of insects during prairie research or monitoring projects. However, despite our lack of comprehensive information, it does appear that higher-diversity plant communities have more species of insects than do poor-quality sites. Many insect species rely on one particular plant species for at least part of their life (egg-laying site, larval feeding, or adult feeding), so the loss of a plant species from a prairie may mean the loss of one or more insect species that rely on it. In addition, insects, like reptiles and amphibians, are ectothermic (cold-blooded) and regulate their temperature by moving to warm and cool places. More-diverse plant communities provide more variety in vegetation structure, and that helps insects move quickly to the microclimate they need at any single time.

Insect Herbivores

Herbivorous insects, those that eat plants, make up the bulk of the insect biomass in prairies. They are a very diverse group. For example, Kansas has more than 300 species of grasshoppers. At Konza Prairie, in the Flint Hills of Kansas, scientists found between 0.6 and 1.2 grams of grasshoppers per square meter of prairie. That might not sound impressive until you compare it to the average biomass of bison spread across that same prairie—1.3 grams per square meter.

Herbivores are very important to the ecology and function of prairies. They can certainly affect plant growth, reproduction, and survival by directly feeding on plants, but they have other less obvious impacts as well. Herbivory speeds up the decomposition rate of vegetation and can increase the nutrient levels of leaf litter on the ground. In addition, herbivores can stimulate increased plant growth by trimming aging roots and leaves, initiating new growth—and that, in turn, increases the rate at which nutrients are pulled from the soil. Finally, some insects, including aphids and leafhoppers, can spread plant viruses and other disease organisms. While the spread of disease might sound like a negative trait, those processes are part of what prevents any single plant species from becoming too abundant.

Some herbivorous insects are generalists, and feed relatively indiscriminately on a number of plant species. Others specialize on one species or a group of species. These insects use either visual or scent cues to help them find the plants they want. Sometimes they cue in on a particular color or shape, other times they are attracted by sugars or amino acids produced by the plants. Ironically, sometimes insects follow the smell of the very chemicals the plants produce to avoid being eaten. As an example, milkweeds produce chemicals called cardenolides that discourage many insects from feeding on them. Those same chemicals, though, are used by monarch butterflies, some aphids, and milkweed beetles to find the plants. Once there, those insects can digest and detoxify the chemicals.

Another important group of herbivores are the seedeaters, or granivores, including species of weevils, beetles, bugs, wasps, ants, thrips, and some moths. Granivores can play a very large role in the reproductive ability of plants by eating all or most of the seeds they produce. However, many seedeaters are also critical for their seed dispersal services. Sometimes seeds are simply knocked from the plant while the insect is feeding, but other times seeds are carried long distances. Seeds can be lost during transport or end up in nests or storage areas where they may be eaten or forgotten. The most effective seed dispersers are ants, which are discussed in detail below.

Among insect pollinators, bees are the most effective at fertilizing flowers. While European honey bees are the best known, there are hundreds of native bee species, like this one, in prairies as well.

Pollinators

About 65 percent of flowering plants require insects for pollination. While most people recognize butterflies and bees as pollinators, many other kinds of insects (and some vertebrates) are important pollinators, including flies, wasps, thrips, moths, true bugs, and some beetles. In general, pollination happens when an insect is feeding on pollen or nectar from a plant and some pollen gets stuck to the insect and transferred to the next flower it feeds on. Most pollinators are nectar feeders and pick up pollen accidentally, and they are the most effective from the plant's point of view. Pollen feeders are less efficient because they eat the pollen they are "supposed to" transfer, or they may not go anywhere near the female organs of the flowers, or they may actually eat the part they are supposed to pollinate.

While many kinds of insects can pollinate flowers, bees are by far the most important because of the way they feed. Bees visit many flowers while collecting pollen to carry home to their nest. Because of this, the chance that a bee will transfer pollen between flowers of the same species is high. The best-known bee is the nonnative honey bee, but there are at least 3,500 species of native bees in North America.

Most bees are thought to be particularly sensitive to habitat fragmentation because they are tied to a nest site and thus have a limited foraging range. Both native bees and honey bees travel out to collect food and then return to a nest. Bumblebees and honey bees, in particular, are active all season long, so they have to find enough food to sustain themselves and their nest throughout that entire time; they must have access to a consistent supply of nectar and pollen within their limited travel range.

Ants

Ants are one of the most numerous insects in prairies, and they also play critical roles in grassland ecosystems. They are major predators, important seed dispersal agents, and soil aerators. High-quality prairies may have around 30 species of ants in them. While that is a respectable number of species, the sheer abundance of ants is the really impressive number. Researchers have estimated their biomass in some prairies to be higher than that of grasshoppers.

All prairie ants eat other insects. They particularly target slow-moving, fleshy insect larvae, like grubs and smooth caterpillars, but will eat anything that's easy to catch and kill. Fuzzy or hard-bodied insects tend to be less susceptible. While ants are smaller than most of their prey, they are extremely efficient predators because of their overwhelming numbers and organization. A roving ant can locate slow-moving prey, send a report back to the colony, and quickly mobilize an impressive force that can kill the prey and transport it back to the colony.

However, ants have a number of other food sources as well, depending upon the species. Ants can raise, or "farm," other insects and extract food from them, raid the nests of other ants for food and/or slaves, or scavenge food from the carcasses of dead animals. Many ants have a sweet tooth. Some ants actually farm sap-feeding insects like aphids. They often keep them in

Ants are tremendously important components of ecosystem functioning in prairies, serving as predators, earthmovers, and seed dispersal agents.

underground caverns where the aphids feed on plant roots. Ants roam the cavern and tap the aphids with their antennae to get them to secrete honey dew, or excess sugars, which the ants feed on. The ants will also periodically slaughter and eat the aphids themselves.

Some plant species take advantage of the sweet tooth of ants by providing them food in return for protection. Sunflowers and partridge peas, for example, attract ants by producing extrafloral nectar from their leaves, stems, or buds. The ants feed on the nectar, but also aggressively defend the plant from other herbivores. The plants expend valuable resources to make the nectar, but may receive far more benefit from the protection service provided by the ants.

Plants can also benefit from the affinity of ants for seeds, in part because many species of ants incorporate plant fragments and seeds into their nests. Ants are particularly valuable as seed dispersers because of their abundance and mobility, and also because they often carry seeds home, eat the fleshy portions, and discard the hard seed in underground trash piles. Those trash areas often provide ideal conditions for germination. Plant species like violets, trout lilies, and certain sedges have fruits that particularly attract ants.

Finally, ants are very important soil movers and aerators. They are especially important in northern prairies where there are no native earthworms, but even further south, ants move more soil than do earthworms. The mounds of spoil at the top of ant tunnels are important too. The soil disturbance creates places for seed germination, and the waste from ant colonies enriches the soil around the mounds. Some other invertebrates also rely exclusively on ant mound habitat, creating a dependent community much like those that spring up in prairie dog towns, in which a number of animals such as burrowing owls, rattlesnakes, black-footed ferrets, and others all assemble around the dogs and their system of burrows.

Predatory Invertebrates

About half of the world's insects eat other insects. Predatory insect groups include mantids, dragonflies, damselflies, lacewings, robberflies, scorpionflies, and others. They can be predatory as adults, larvae, or both. There are also a large number of other invertebrate predators like spiders, centipedes, and scorpions. Some of those predators are generalists and some are specialists. Some, like hornets and tiger beetles, catch their prey with pure speed. Others, like ambush bugs and crab spiders, sit and wait to grab unsuspecting prey. Many are larger than their prey, but others, like ants, can overwhelm with numbers. Invertebrate predators usually either dismember their prey with strong biting or chewing mouthparts or inject them with fluid to paralyze them and liquefy their tissues before sucking them dry. Regardless of their methods, predators play a critically important role in regulating populations of other insects.

Crab spiders like this one lie in wait on flowers for pollinators or other small insects to come within reach of their long front legs. Many can change color (e.g., from white to yellow) to match the color of the flower they're on.

Parasites and Parasitoids

A particularly gruesome assemblage of insects is that of the parasites and parasitoids, which comprise about 15 percent of all insects. Parasites live at the expense of a living host organism. Some parasites, like lice, live on the outside of their host's body, while others, like tapeworms, live inside them. Still others, like mosquitoes, feed on their hosts only periodically. Fleas, ticks, mites, leeches, and some kinds of worms and flies are also parasites.

Parasitoids lead lives straight out of a horror movie. The adults lay eggs either on or inside a living host insect. When the eggs hatch, the larvae begin feeding on the host until it eventually dies. Some parasitoids paralyze the prey before it is eaten alive, but others do not. Parasitoids include tachinid flies and a number of wasps. Just like predators, parasites and parasitoids play important roles as regulators of population size in nature. Their methods may seem creepy or distasteful, but we'd miss them if they were gone.

Insect Decomposers

Some insects aid in decomposition by feeding on dead or dying plant tissue, dead animals, or animal feces. The importance of their role in an ecosystem is pretty clear—it doesn't take much imagination to picture what the world would look like without decomposers. Insects that feed on dead plants accelerate decay by increasing the surface area of the plant that is exposed to weathering and the action of other decomposers. This group of insects is largely responsible for making humus, the upper layer of organic matter in soil. Insects that scavenge from dead animals are also an important part of the decomposition process. Common scavengers are the larvae of flies (maggots), and some wasps, mites, and ants. Finally, dung-feeders like flies and dung beetles lay eggs on fresh feces, and their larvae feed on the organic matter. Many times, an insect species will specialize on the feces of a particular animal species or group of species.

Grassland Birds

Almost everyone knows what a meadowlark looks like. But many people would be hard pressed to name or describe any of the other species of birds that nest in grasslands. Grassland nesting birds are a diverse and extremely interesting group of birds, but they suffer from public relations problems because most have dull coloring, they tend to hide in the grass, and they live in places that most people just drive past without stopping. Because they are largely ignored by the public, that same public is largely unaware that grassland bird populations are declining faster than any other group of birds worldwide.

It's really quite easy to like grassland birds once you get to know them. They include some of the most interesting birds in the world. Prairie-chickens are well known for their "booming" during spring courtship rituals, in which the males dance around on short-cropped hilltops making unearthly music in the

hope of impressing the females that watch from the sidelines. Upland sandpipers are tall pencil-necked shorebirds, often seen perching on fenceposts and power poles. Their call, made while they circle around in the air on long skinny wings, sounds like a construction worker whistling at a pretty woman. Bobolinks are starkly black-and-white birds that sound exactly like R2-D2 from *Star Wars*; dickcissels look like sparrow-sized meadowlarks; sedge wrens sound like little machine guns as they defend their territories like soldiers; and the rare Henslow's sparrows are a big treat for serious birders to see because the only sound they make is a short, quiet, little chipping call, usually made while hiding in tall grass. What's not to like?

Some grassland birds suspend their nests several feet off the ground in grasses or low shrubs, but the majority build simple nests right on the ground. Either way, they are essentially relying on the needle-in-a-haystack strategy for survival. They're betting that if they put a small grassy nest in the middle of a large grassy area, predators will not be able to find them. Overall, it's not a bad strategy, but it works less effectively when the haystack —the prairie—gets really small. Predators of grassland birds and their chicks and

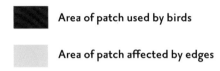

Area of patch used by birds

Area of patch affected by edges

Figure 5. The shape of a habitat patch can be important to grassland birds. The two patches shown in this illustration are of equal size, but the long skinny patch has much less area for nesting away from the edge.

eggs include everything from snakes and skunks to thirteen-lined ground squirrels. Even white-tailed deer have been seen eating grassland bird nestlings. Those numerous predators can find many more of the nests in a small prairie than they can in a large open prairie. Since many predators live on the edges of prairies, the further a nest is from an edge, the safer it tends to be.

In addition to predators, grassland birds are vulnerable to brood parasitism from brown-headed cowbirds. Cowbirds, a native species in grasslands, lay their eggs in the nests of other bird species and let those other parents raise their young. Because cowbirds generally hatch first and grow faster and larger than the host young, they tend to monopolize the food delivered by the parents. Often, a grasshopper sparrow or meadowlark will end up struggling to provide enough food to satisfy a hungry cowbird or three, while their own young die of starvation. In addition, cowbird mothers will sometimes remove host eggs from the nest as they lay theirs to help tip the odds further in favor of the cowbird chicks. Some grassland birds will abandon nests if they see cowbird eggs, but their greater protection is the same as with predators— hide the nest in the middle of a large area and hope it's not found.

Grassland birds are a diverse group of species, and their habitat needs for nesting are equally diverse. Birds like upland sandpipers and horned larks like to nest in very short grass, while dickcissels, Henslow's sparrows, and sedge wrens prefer tall, rank vegetation. Grasshopper sparrows, one of the most common but most overlooked of the grassland birds, can live in a variety of grassland structure types, but seem to prefer heavily grazed pastures. Meadowlarks like their grass pretty short, but eastern meadowlarks tend to nest in moister areas while western meadowlarks go for drier sites. Bobolinks can live in a variety of habitats but are commonly found in hay meadows and alfalfa fields, which start out short but get taller as the season progresses.

In addition to their requirements for various kinds of vegetation structure, grassland birds are well known for being sensitive to the size and shape of prairies (figure 5). Many species will not nest in prairies less than 40 acres in size, and it's rare to see a really diverse mix of grassland bird species in a prairie of less than 100 acres. In addition to being picky about habitat patch size, grassland birds tend not to like nesting in skinny prairie patches. This all makes perfect sense when you remember their needle-in-a-haystack approach to nesting. It's hard to hide a nest successfully in a 5-acre haymeadow, and even a 100-acre prairie doesn't work well if it's long and skinny, because most of a skinny prairie is close to its edges—where predators tend to patrol.

In addition to a fear of predators, grassland bird sensitivity to prairie edges may also be related to their social behavior. Grassland birds are very territorial. They, like most other birds, sing to advertise their dominance in their own territory. In addition, males regularly fly from perch to perch around the edges of their territory, always watching the birds on surrounding territories to make sure they aren't trying to grab land or steal their females. In fact, it's pretty easy to figure out the size and shape of a grassland bird's territory just by flushing it a few times and watching where it will and won't fly. Normally, it stays within a very well-defined area because its neighbors are defending their own territories against it and because it can't afford to leave its territory for a minute—even in the face of a big scary person chasing it around.

While biologists are sure that most prairie birds avoid the edges of prairies, we are still learning about what actually constitutes an edge and what kinds of edges are worse than others. Trees can definitely have a negative impact on habitat use by grassland birds. Many research projects have documented grassland birds staying far away from wooded edges of prairies, and even

Even scattered trees can greatly affect the habitat availability for nesting grassland birds.

from isolated trees or small groves in the center of a prairie. Because of this, trees in or around the edges of prairies actually make those prairies much smaller in the eyes of grassland birds. A 100-acre prairie surrounded by trees and with scattered groves around the middle of it might contain only a few species of birds, but clearing the trees away can attract many of the more sensitive species almost instantly. Cropland edges seem to be less of a problem for grassland birds, perhaps because they don't block visibility and do provide feeding areas. A new potential threat to grassland birds is an increasing number of wind turbines in grassland landscapes. Recent research has shown that turbines, along with the roads and power lines that accompany them, have a significant impact on habitat use by grassland birds, and that impact can extend up to a mile or more from each turbine. More research, focusing on various kinds of edges and the way grassland birds respond to them, will continue to clarify the impact of habitat fragmentation. But there's no question that large, open prairies attract the largest complement of grassland bird species, and that those birds tend to breed more successfully in those conditions as well.

Greater prairie-chickens are often mentioned during discussions of prairie fragmention. Many biologists think prairie-chickens are important because they require relatively large and varied habitats, thus acting as a kind of umbrella species from a management perspective. The idea is that a landscape that meets the needs of prairie-chickens will likely meet the needs of the majority of other grassland species as well. Whether or not this is true is still being debated, but it is certainly true that it takes a particular range of conditions to attract and maintain a healthy prairie-chicken population.

Prairie-chicken habitat needs vary by season. During the winter, they need tall dense cover, particularly tall clumps of warm-season grasses that can provide shelter from cold winds and snow. In the spring, males seek out hilltops with short-cropped grass for their display grounds, and then, after mating, females go to patches of moderately dense vegetation to nest. Those nesting areas have to be dense enough to hide a nest but not so dense that they prevent hens from seeing approaching predators. Once the chicks hatch, they are mobile right away, and the female leads them to habitat where they can catch insects, their primary food, under protective cover. Ideal brood-rearing habitat is interspersed with nesting habitat and consists of forb-dominated vegetation that is open enough at the ground level that chicks can run freely to catch insects and escape predators, but that also has enough overhead cover to hide them from predators. Cropfields are also used by chickens, particularly during the winter. In addition to all of this, prairie-chickens tend to be sensitive to the encroachment of trees (and other visibility-obstructing structures like wind turbines and power lines) on the landscape. Wooded draws seem to be acceptable, but trees growing high on hillsides or hilltops can make otherwise suitable grassland unusable.

Prairie-chickens have disappeared from many of the tallgrass and mixed-grass prairies. Even if they aren't a perfect umbrella species, they are certainly a good example of the effects of a fragmented prairie landscape. In some areas, federal and state-sponsored conservation programs (like the Conservation Reserve Program, or CRP) have helped to draw chickens back to some landscapes, but those populations may or may not be stable, and they rely on temporary subsidies to farmers to replace cropland with grassland. Even in those landscapes, active management of vegetation structure is needed to provide the suite of habitat conditions required by prairie-chickens.

Bobwhite quail are native grassland birds that require many of the same habitats as prairie-chickens, with two major exceptions. First, quail don't have the kind of spring mating displays chickens do, and so don't require that kind of open habitat. Second, and more important, quail have a strong need for dense shrubby vegetation. Shrub patches act as kind of a home base for coveys (groups) of quail and can provide safe harbor from both predators and heavy snows.

Ring-necked pheasants are nonnative birds, but because of their popularity as hunting targets they have become the most visible grassland wildlife species for many people. Pheasants have habitat requirements very similar to those of prairie-chickens and bobwhite quail except that they don't require spring mating display habitat and aren't tied strongly to shrubby habitat. In addition, pheasants use taller, denser vegetation to hide from predators than do the other two species.

Reptiles and Amphibians

Reptiles and amphibians are common but often overlooked inhabitants of prairies. Most are small but important predators in prairie ecosystems, consuming large quantities of insects and other prey. In upland prairies, you can often find box turtles, numerous species of snakes, and an occasional lizard. Closer to water, you may also see several species of toads and frogs, and tiger salamanders. Amphibians (toads, frogs, and salamanders) all start their lives in water and need access to water or moist soil as adults to keep from drying out. During extended droughts, many will aestivate, or go into long periods of inactivity, until moisture returns. Reptiles are more independent of moist areas and can live in very dry habitats. Both reptiles and amphibians, though, are ectothermic (cold-blooded). Their need to regulate their body temperature by moving to warm or cool places governs their habitat needs. Habitats with patchy vegetation structure, including areas of bare ground or sparse

grass interspersed with denser vegetation, give them the best opportunities to optimize their body temperature.

In addition, many reptiles and amphibians travel from one habitat type to another each season. Water-dwelling turtles, for example, leave the water to find upland sites to bury their eggs. Many species of snakes spend the winter in hibernacula such as deep crevices in rocky ledges, where large numbers of snakes huddle together to keep warm. Some will travel long distances each year between the hibernacula and their summer habitats. Other snake species, including water snakes, some garter snakes, and massasauga rattlesnakes, spend their winters underground in crayfish burrows, sometimes hibernating underwater. Traveling from one habitat to another has always made reptiles and amphibians vulnerable to predation, but, more recently, habitat fragmentation has increased their risks. Roads, in particular, are a major cause of mortality to migrating reptiles and amphibians, but cropfields, lawns, and other human-altered landscapes now either prevent animals from moving between habitats or greatly increase the risk of travel.

Snakes are the most common and diverse group of reptiles in prairies. While they certainly stimulate strong feelings of fear or dislike in some people, the vast majority of snakes are harmless to people and very rarely seen. There are only a few venomous snakes in the midwestern United States, and they all have limited geographic distributions. Cottonmouths are the only poisonous water snake, and they are found only in the far southern portion of the prairies. All rattlesnakes in central North America have rattles on the tips of their tails, making them easy to identify—even very small rattlesnakes have little button rattles. Rattlesnakes have disappeared from most tallgrass and mixed-grass prairie areas, however, so, depending upon your location, they may or may not be a concern.

Aside from the few poisonous snakes there are many other kinds, varying greatly in size, coloring, and habits. There are a few large ones, like bullsnakes, which can reach lengths of over 6 feet, but most are much smaller, ranging from less than the length of a pencil to a couple feet. These include several species of garter snakes in addition to racers, corn snakes, milk snakes, brown snakes, ring-necked snakes, hognosed snakes, and many others. Larger snakes may need to catch and eat only a few large animals a year, while smaller snakes need frequent meals of insects, tadpoles, or other small creatures.

Mammals

Mammals may be the most familiar group of animals, but in practice few of them are seen in prairies. The biggest are the bison (and now cattle) that are discussed in more detail elsewhere in this book. Many of the other large mammals, including bears, wolves, elk, mule deer, pronghorn, and mountain lions, have been pushed out of most prairie landscapes by habitat fragmentation and human influence. A few, like mountain lions and elk, are now slowly moving back into some areas. White-tailed deer numbers have gone in the opposite direction, and deer are now dramatically more abundant than they were in pre-European–settlement times. High deer numbers and the lack of sufficient predator pressure have wreaked havoc on the forb populations of many small prairies. Deer thrive in mixed habitats of trees, grassland, and cropfields, and like to feed near woody cover. Prairies that don't have large open areas well away from wooded edges can suffer very high browsing rates on many forb species.

Most prairie mammals, of course, are much smaller than deer and bison.

The most numerous are the smallest, including mice and voles, which are rarely seen except for brief glimpses as they scoot away through the grass. The best evidence of their presence is normally found in the winter, when their trails and burrows can be easily seen in the snow. In addition, voles make runways through the prairie litter right at the surface of the ground. These runways allow them to navigate quickly through even relatively dense grass, to escape predators and to forage efficiently. Other species of small mammals, particularly mice, take advantage of vole runways as well.

There are many species of small mammals in prairies, and while they intermix with each other, each species tends to have its own habitat structure preferences. Some, like the western harvest mouse, prefer open grasslands, while others, like the white-footed mouse, prefer to be near or under shrubby or woody cover. Many, including harvest mice, cotton rats, and shrews, prefer areas where litter has been allowed to build up over multiple years, while still others, like the deer mouse, do very well in recently burned habitat. Most of these small mammals are omnivorous, eating green shoots and leaves in the summer and seeds in the winter, but supplementing their diet with insects, fungi, roots, and tubers. Exceptions to this include grasshopper mice, which eat primarily insects, and shrews, which eat primarily worms and other invertebrates.

As a group, small mammals consume a very significant amount of vegetation in grasslands, especially if some of the slightly larger mammals like ground squirrels, cottontails, and jack rabbits are included. Both cottontails and jack rabbits eat mainly green vegetation, but, along with voles, they will also eat the tender bark from young trees during the winter. While this behavior is irritating to landowners trying to establish new trees, it is probably an important process that helps prevent excessive invasion of prairies by trees and shrubs.

One very important role that some mammals play is the creation of burrows. Prairie dogs are the most famous prairie burrowers, though their range is mainly west of the geographic scope of this book. There are, however, a number of other burrowing mammals, including badgers, coyotes, foxes, pocket gophers, moles, ground squirrels, and others. These diggers

Most small mammals are difficult to see during the majority of the year, but winter snows provide evidence of their abundance and activity.

are important for several reasons. First, they create soil disturbance that can increase soil aeration and water infiltration. More important, those disturbances create space for colonizing plants. In many prairies where grazing and other intense disturbances no longer occur, the creation of bare soil by mammals can be extremely important for those short-lived plants. Lastly, the burrows and tunnels created by these mammals become homes, shelters, and/or transportation corridors for other species, including snakes, spiders, burrowing owls, rabbits, mice, and many others. Most of those species rely on mammal burrows because they are unable to dig their own.

Predators

Predators in prairies play a critical role in regulating their prey populations, but their impact is broader than the direct thinning of population. The mere presence of predators in a landscape changes the behavior of prey species, altering the location and timing of their feeding and also the food they choose. However, predatory animals are often unpopular with the people who live in the same landscapes with them, and considerable effort goes into their control and removal. In many agricultural areas, predators are seen as threats to livestock. Hunters and other wildlife enthusiasts blame predators for low numbers of pheasants, turkey, deer, or other game species. As a result, predator control has become entrenched in our culture. The hunting and trapping of predators is done both to benefit livestock production and as pure sport.

Unfortunately, while intensive predator control has been going on for well over a century, there is little conclusive data to support any benefits from it—either to livestock production or game species. In fact, from as far back as the 1940s, biologists like Aldo Leopold and others have demonstrated the negative impacts of predator control efforts. The absence of large predators allows their prey species populations to grow much larger and leads to detrimental impacts to an ecosystem not adapted to those numbers. In addition, many indirect responses to low predator numbers are being documented, including the following example from Yellowstone.

One of the best-known and controversial predators in North America is the gray wolf. The recent reintroduction of wolves into Yellowstone National Park has stimulated a great deal of discussion about whether or not humans and large predators can coexist in the same landscape. While wolves have been absent from tallgrass and mixed-grass prairie for more than a hundred years, studies of the Yellowstone reintroduction provide some intriguing information about how the presence of wolves and other large predators can influence an ecosystem.

When wolves were reintroduced into Yellowstone, scientists expected to see an increase in predation on species such as elk, but they found a much more complex interaction, now called the ecology of fear. What the scientists found was that the presence of wolves in Yellowstone Park has influenced the way elk choose feeding sites. Elk now avoid feeding along streams, where they feel particularly vulnerable to wolf predation, allowing a recovery of aspen, cottonwood, and willow species which had been in severe decline since the 1920s (when wolves were exterminated from the park). The study at Yellowstone has now been replicated in other locations and the same impacts have been seen. The fear of large predators forces prey species to choose safer feeding locations, and that can have huge implications that cascade through the ecosystem. For example, the recovery of willows along streambanks can increase populations of other species, including neotropical birds, fish, amphibians, insects, and beaver. The increase in beaver populations in those areas can have an impact upon other aspects of the ecosystem, including sediment retention, wetland maintenance, and nutrient cycling—which leads to an overall increase in biological diversity.

To make the story even more interesting, research shows that wolves are also helping to stabilize the boom-and-bust population cycles of elk. Elk numbers have historically been tied to conditions during the winter. Severe winters caused declines in the population, and short, warm winters allowed elk numbers to rise. Aside from the impact on vegetation eaten by elk, the instability in elk numbers affected the availability of food for scavenging animals, including bears, coyotes, ravens, and eagles. During mild winters, little food was available for these animals, but the presence of wolves has meant that elk are killed more regularly through the winter, regardless of the severity of the weather. As an added benefit, wolves tend to "share" their food with scavengers much more readily than do the other top predators (bears and mountain lions), which either hide or guard their kills. Scientists speculate that this increased stability of food availability will become even more important as impending climate change causes shorter, milder winters in the future.

The impact that a relatively small number of wolves have had in a large landscape like Yellowstone National Park provides food for thought for those of us in the prairie region of North America, where sky-high deer populations cause crop losses, collisions with automobiles, and declines in prairie wildflower populations. The reintroduction of wolves into the eastern Great Plains isn't practical from the standpoint of either wolves or humans—the fragmented habitat and extensive human presence on the landscape prevent the discussion from even getting started. But there are predators that can survive in the current landscape. One of the most successful and important is the coyote. Although coyotes don't always have a positive reputation, they are a critical part of the grassland ecosystem. Coyotes are really the only significant nonhuman predator of deer left in most prairies. They take fawns primarily, but can also kill weakened adults, especially during the winter. Besides the role they play in controlling the populations of deer, small mammals, and other prey species, they help to keep other predator populations in check. Species such as raccoons, skunks, and foxes increase their numbers dramatically when coyotes become scarce.

Other important large predators in prairies include bobcats and, increasingly, mountain lions. Mountain lions are slowly reappearing in many landscapes, particularly in the mixed-grass prairie and western tallgrass prairie. It is not yet certain what the future of those populations will be. Lions in fragmented landscapes will interact with humans more frequently than they do in larger western landscapes. Balancing the potential ecological benefits of mountain lions, and their appeal to some people, with the safety of the human and livestock populations will be an interesting challenge. Bobcats are already relatively common, if rarely seen, predators in much of the prairie region. Because they are rarely seen and not well studied, their impact is not well known.

Raptors (hawks, eagles, falcons, and owls) and other avian predators are also an important factor in prairies. They eat mainly small mammals and snakes, though they will also feed on other small animals, including insects. Although not well studied, there is certainly a relationship between the pres-

Opossums are one of many grassland predators that have benefited from the increase in wooded edges throughout the prairie regions of North America. They have a varied diet that includes insects and small mammals.

ence of those raptors in a landscape and the response of their prey, including their movement and feeding patterns. As one example, we have seen that mice feed much more on prairie forb seeds in areas of dense vegetation cover than in short-cropped prairie. We assume that the mice are taking advantage of the cover from owls and other predators. Regardless, the result is that forbs that don't get grazed off by cattle, but are in shorter vegetation, will drop more seed than those in tall dense vegetation. Interestingly, those seeds that drop in the more heavily grazed areas also have a better chance of germinating since the surrounding vegetation has been suppressed by grazing. So plants in grazed areas are less susceptible to having their seeds eaten by mice and also have a better chance of their seeds germinating—and this is all tied to the fact that mice respond to the presence of owls and other predators. Removing predators from a complex relationship like this is likely to have a far-reaching impact.

While many raptors are active predators in prairies, only a few are actually grassland nesters. The vast majority nest in trees in or around the edge of prairies, including species like red-tailed hawks, great horned owls, and kestrels. The most common true grassland-nesting raptors in midwestern prairies are the northern harriers. However, in many prairies they are seen only during spring and fall migration because they typically require very large, open grassland areas for nesting. In those large grasslands, they build a nest right on the ground like any other grassland bird. While they are much smaller than red-tailed hawks, harriers appear to be much larger than they actually are because of their extremely long wings. Those wings facilitate their characteristic hunting technique of gliding slowly and gracefully back and forth across a prairie, often just above the tips of tall grasses. They feed mainly on small prey like voles but will take rabbits and small birds as well, capturing the birds mainly by surprise while they are perched rather than in the air.

There are many smaller species of predatory mammals and reptiles in prairies too, including raccoons, skunks, opossums, weasels, foxes, badgers, and a number of snake species. In addition to being direct predators of small mammals, birds, and insects, many of these are also nest predators, searching for and consuming eggs and nestlings. As mentioned above, the loss of larger predators has resulted in a significant increase in the abundance of these smaller predators, a phenomenon referred to as mesopredator release. Many of these predators are more abundant now than they may have been historically because of increased habitat fragmentation. Most of them rely heavily on wooded edges for habitat, and the increase in woody habitat has exposed much more grassland area to predation pressure from them.

4. The Importance of Diversity and Heterogeneity

One of the most important components of any healthy and viable ecosystem is diversity. Diversity is strongly linked to the resilience of natural communities. A diverse mix of species in a community, for example, increases the chance that the loss of one species can be somewhat compensated for by other species that might play a similar role in the ecosystem. There are many ways to look at diversity in an ecosystem. Here we'll concentrate on habitat structure diversity and species diversity.

Habitat Structure Diversity

The physical structure of habitat is very important in determining which species can use it. Excluding geologically formed structure types such as lakes, hills, and plains, most habitat structure that affects species is related to vegetation. Forests have much different vegetation structure than shortgrass prairies do, and thus have very different plant and animal species living in them. But the diversity of the structure, both vertically and horizontally, within a forest or prairie is also very important. Heterogeneity refers to the variety of habitat structure available, and, in general, the more heterogeneous the habitat is, the more species will be present.

Vertical structure in a prairie is determined by the kinds of plants present and their respective heights. Forests can have distinct layers of vertical struc-

ture, including litter (leaves and sticks on the ground), herbaceous understory plants, shrubby understory plants, a subcanopy of small trees, and the canopy of mature trees. Prairies don't have layers that are as distinct as those in a forest, but the layers are there nonetheless.

If a prairie has not been burned recently, there is a layer of litter, or thatch, consisting of dead leaves and stems from grasses and forbs. Poking through that litter are numerous species of short-stature grasses and forbs that bloom in the early part of the season when the taller plants they compete with for light are also short. Those later-season tall plants form the top layer of vegetation structure as they tower over the shorter species. When there are multiple years' worth of vegetation present, including the green growth of the current year and the dead stems from previous years, vegetation structure becomes even more complex. Old growth of tall grasses and forbs often falls over, or gets stomped down or knocked over, effectively forming lean-to tents that redirect rainfall, block sunlight, and provide cover for many animals.

Horizontal vegetation structure is a measure of the variation in vertical structure from one part of a prairie to the next. It can be measured on a small or large scale. For example, one prairie might have a very patchy vegetation structure in which a person walking across the prairie might step on nearly bare ground with one foot and tall rank vegetation with the next across the whole site. Another prairie might have uniformly tall vegetation on a large portion of the site, but uniformly short and/or midheight vegetation on the rest. And, of course, many prairies have a combination of both, creating additional heterogeneity.

The diversity and heterogeneity of both vertical and horizontal structure plays a large role in determining which plant and animal species thrive in a prairie. Obviously, if every species has its own requirement for habitat, more kinds of vegetation structure should allow more species to live there. But it is more complicated than that. Some plant species grow well in the shade of other plants and benefit from the cooler conditions there. Other plants need to have open space around and above them to meet both heat and water requirements. In order for a prairie to allow both kinds of plants to survive, it

Grazing can create excellent heterogeneity in vegetation structure because cattle and other large herbivores are selective feeders, eating some plants but leaving others ungrazed. This creates a pattern of short and tall vegetation that provides opportunities for many animals that require both habitat types.

must provide both kinds of habitat structure. And the best-case scenario is to have the vegetation structure in any one place change frequently so that both kinds of plants can survive in any one place, even if they have favorable conditions only periodically.

Animals are more complicated in their habitat structure requirements because they move from place to place to meet their various needs. For example, many insect and reptile species are dependent on being able to regulate their temperature throughout the day and across seasons. On cool mornings, they might want to sit out in direct sunlight to warm up, but then move into the shade during the hot part of the day. And when a cool wind is blowing, they might like to sit in a sunny spot surrounded by thick vegetation that breaks the wind. The more choices provided within the small area traveled by each insect or reptile, the better it will do.

Many other kinds of animals need to nest or sleep in thick vegetation but feed in open areas. If only one type of structure is available, those species won't stick around. Even if multiple types of vegetation structure are present, the size of each structurally similar patch, the distance between patches, and the kind of habitat that separates them are all critical. A small mammal that nests in an area of dense litter might need to feed in a nearby area where the plants are tall enough to hide it from predators but where the litter is thin enough that it can run quickly to escape if necessary. It would be very risky for that small mammal to cross a large area of very short vegetation (where it's completely exposed to predators) to get from one habitat to the other. Prairie-chickens, as discussed earlier, are a great example of a species that needs a variety of habitat structures close to each other. Within the same small landscape, they need short-cropped leks (breeding display sites), dense cover for nesting, and an area with some tall vegetation but sparse understory for successfully rearing their chicks.

Maximizing the number of plant and animal species in a prairie, then, is dependent upon maximizing the types of vegetation structure available. Unfortunately, it's impossible to know the requirements of every species that might use the prairie, and not feasible to provide for all of them at the same time anyway. But consciously considering what kinds of vegetation structure are available, how heterogeneous that structure is across the prairie, and how

Prairie A   ## Prairie B

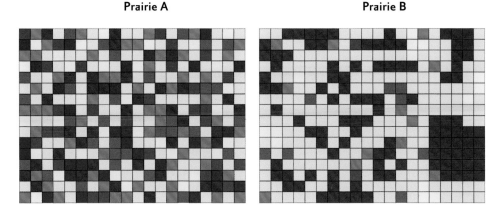

Figure 6. Colors represent individual species and their presence scattered across prairies A and B.

large each patch is will help. On large sites, it is possible to change the kinds of vegetation structure available in any one place each year, and still maintain a good variety across the whole prairie. This will provide the needed habitat for a variety of animals, but also allow for a diversity of plants to survive across the whole site. The next chapter of this book, "Landscape Context," will discuss all of this in more detail.

Species Diversity

Consider two prairies that each contain numerous plant species (figure 6). In prairie A, those species are all relatively abundant and well distributed across the site. In prairie B, a handful of the species are dominant and most of the other species are represented by only a couple plants each. Both prairies have a high number of species (also called species richness). But prairie A has better evenness, meaning that the abundance of the species is more equal.

Species diversity is a measure comprised of both richness and evenness. Even though prairies A and B both have the same richness, prairie A has a higher species diversity because of the relative abundance of each of the species there. Plant species diversity is extremely important for many aspects of prairie health. First, it affects vegetation structure, which, as just discussed, has a long list of impacts. Greater plant species diversity increases the diversity of vegetation structure, even when the vegetation is being managed with homogenizing strategies like mowing. A mowed prairie with lots of different plants is more structurally diverse than a mowed bluegrass yard, even if they are both mowed to the same height.

Besides influencing habitat structure, plant diversity affects animal diversity in other ways as well. One example is the relationship between insect species and their host plant species. In many cases, a particular insect species will feed exclusively on one kind of plant, especially when the insect is in its larval stage. Sometimes, an insect species will lay its eggs and feed its larvae on one species of plant, and use another species or group of species for feeding as an adult. In this way, the diversity of insects—and the abundance of insects—is directly linked to plant diversity.

Many animal species need to shift their feeding from one plant species or group of species to others as the season progresses. One example of this is found in pollinating insects. Many native social bees rely on being able to find dependable sources of nectar and pollen from early spring until late fall. Because each species of wildflower blooms only for a small portion of the season, those bees need to have a diverse group of flowering plant species available within the small area (often a square mile or so) surrounding their nest. To make it even more complicated, most bee species are adapted to use only certain shapes and sizes of flowers, so having any old flower species blooming at a particular time is not good enough. To allow the entire diversity of bee species to survive, the entire diversity of bee-pollinated flowers has to be present too—and abundant enough to provide sufficient nectar and pollen. The lack of dependable pollen and nectar supplies due to a low diversity of flowering plants can lead to an ever-worsening downward spiral, because fewer pollinators result in less reproduction and survival of flower species, and that can lower plant diversity even more.

Plant diversity is important for herbivores as well as for pollinators. Specialist herbivores, which feed on only one or a select group of plant species, are obviously dependent upon those species being sufficiently abundant. But many more generalist herbivores also rely on plant diversity to help them

Prairies with high plant diversity also provide important heterogeneity in habitat structure because of the varied architecture of each plant species.

regulate their nutritional needs through the season. Less plant-species diversity means fewer choices for the herbivores, and a greater possibility of not finding an adequate food supply during some part of the year. An extreme example would be if a prairie was dominated almost exclusively by smooth brome or some other cool-season grass. Grass-feeding herbivores would be unable to subsist during the long hot summer when that cool-season grass was dormant and warm-season grasses were not abundant enough to sustain them. But even in less extreme cases, herbivores (including cattle) generally need to be able to choose between a variety of plant species and/or types to ensure that they meet their nutritional requirements. Herbivores are very good at being able to recognize when their diet is lacking in minor minerals or other nutrients, and they can find and eat plants that help remedy that. The more plant species in a prairie, the more likely it is that herbivores will be able to choose a healthy and sustaining diet.

A diversity of food sources is important for carnivorous animals as well. They need a consistent supply of insects and/or other prey animals to sustain themselves through the year. Again, a high diversity of prey species means that it is likely that there will always be something for carnivores to eat. If there were only a few prey species in a prairie, any up-and-down cycling in their population numbers would have a great impact on the animals that feed on them. But a diverse prey community smooths out those highs and lows in the food supply. In a year when some species are experiencing population declines, the populations of other species are likely to be higher than normal, providing a more or less constant supply of prey for animals that feed on them. And, of course, because most of those prey species rely on a diverse plant community, carnivores do too.

Some recent studies have shown that more-diverse plant communities resist invasive species better than less-diverse communities. While this is still being debated and tested, it is almost certainly true in at least some extreme cases. A Conservation Reserve Program (CRP) field planted to just a few species of warm-season grasses will not always remain a pure stand of those grasses. Because those grasses grow only during the hot part of the growing season, it can be relatively easy for cool-season plants, such as smooth brome or Kentucky bluegrass, to invade. The cool-season grass can get started in the fall and/or spring when moisture is available and not being used up by the warm-season grasses. In years when the spring is wet and the summer is dry (a common scenario in prairie regions), those cool-season grasses gain a distinct advantage because they monopolize the spring moisture and leave nothing but dry soil all summer for the warm-season grasses. It seems reasonable to expect that there would be similar occurrences in other examples of low-diversity plant communities where the existing community does not monopolize the available resources, leaving the door open for invasive species.

If invasion resistance really is tied to community diversity, another reason for that resistance is probably the redundancy in function found in diverse systems. In a very diverse prairie, there are many overlaps between plant species that use similar resources and/or fill similar roles. For example, there might be a handful of small-stature legumes that fix nitrogen, have similar rooting depths, and bloom in April and May. If one of those species is attacked by a disease or outbreak of insects in a particular year, or even driven out of a particular prairie by repeated attacks, many of the services provided to the prairie by that species would be covered by other, similar species. There would certainly be impacts from losing that species, especially if there were insect species that required it as a larval host. But generalist herbivores and pollinators that normally used that plant at a particular time of year would likely survive just fine—as long as only that one species was lost. There are many examples of this kind of ecological resilience that is tied to species diversity. Prairies with higher levels of resilience are more likely to respond successfully to severe disturbances such as drought, severe grazing, insect or disease outbreaks, or combinations of all of those. Not only will diverse communities have community members ready to expand their abundance in response to those disturbances (e.g., colonizer plants), but they are also likely to respond in a way that continues to repel invasive species.

All habitats are arranged in patches. Grasslands, croplands, woodlands, urban areas, and bodies of water are all examples of habitat patches. It's usually difficult to see from the ground the way those patches are arranged, but from the air you can see patterns resembling the patchwork design of a quilt. The way that any landscape "quilt" is designed affects the movement and survival of all the organisms that live there. In this chapter we'll look at four characteristics of an ecological landscape, all of them dealing with habitat patches. Those characteristics are size, shape and exposure to edges, layout, and connectivity.

Patch Size

The size of a habitat patch can have a big influence on the kinds of animals and plants that can use it. Many animals have minimum size needs for their home range (the area they cover while searching for food and for filling other needs). Some highly adaptable species like deer have large home ranges, but those can include a variety of habitat patches, so the size of each patch is less important. However, many other species live only in grasslands and need a patch of prairie large enough to provide everything they need to survive. Most grassland-nesting birds, including bobolinks, upland sandpipers, meadowlarks, and grasshopper sparrows, seem to have minimum requirements for the size of prairie they are willing to nest in. That minimum requirement varies by species, but to host a diverse community of grassland bird species, a prairie generally has to be at least 100 acres in size.

The size of a patch can also determine the likelihood that animals and plants will maintain a population over time. Larger patches can support larger populations of animals and plants, which gives them a better ability to survive reductions in population. As an example, take a population of an imaginary butterfly species ("red-spotted flitters") in a 100-acre prairie surrounded by cropland. Let's say the 100-acre prairie can support a population of about 1,000 adult flitters. This imaginary butterfly species depends on a single imaginary species of plant ("false skunkweed") because that's where flitters lay their eggs and it's what they feed on while they're caterpillars. Flitters and skunkweed, like all living things, are subject to predation, disease, impacts from weather, and other dangers. A bad year for flitters in that 100-acre prairie might go something like this: 50 percent of the skunkweed plants they lay eggs on wither in a drought, allowing only 500 caterpillars to survive to adulthood (instead of 1,000); and then 50 percent of the surviving adult butterflies (250 out of 500) get eaten by birds. So in that bad year only 250 adult flitters survive to lay eggs. Because flitters can lay lots of eggs, the population might rebound pretty quickly if the next year is better, but it might take longer if the drought continues.

Losing three-fourths of a population in one year is pretty tough, but it's even tougher when the population is small to begin with. If the prairie was only 10 acres and the same scenario occurred, only 25 flitters might survive and lay eggs that year. The chance that those 25 butterflies would lay enough eggs to ensure that at least a few survive to adulthood is much lower than the chance would be if you started with 250 butterflies. That means that a single bad year in a small prairie could spell the end of that flitter population altogether. And if the red-spotted flitter is like most real species of prairie butterflies, the likelihood that any adventurous flitter would accidentally find and recolonize that isolated 10-acre prairie in the future is very small.

Patch Shape and Exposure to Edges

The shape of a habitat patch affects its exposure to forces outside that patch. The negative impacts on animals and plants related to the edge of a habitat

Trees and shrubs along fencelines, roads, and other edges of prairies can have negative impacts on nesting grassland birds and many other prairie animals. They also provide abundant seed sources from which aggressive tree species can invade prairies.

patch are called edge effects. Edge effects can include increased predation rates, microclimate differences, and encroachment of weeds, trees, or other invasive species.

Limiting the amount of edge a prairie is exposed to can increase the health of its grassland communities. Circular patches have much less edge per unit area than long skinny patches, and larger patches have less edge per unit area than smaller patches of the same shape. So a large round prairie is better off than a small skinny prairie. The type of habitat along the edge of a prairie can be important as well. For example, wooded edges tend to be more dangerous to prairie species than cropland or other softer edges because of the difference in structure (a cornfield is much more like a grassland than a forest is). Finally, edge effects can radiate from "holes" punched in the center of a prairie too, so eliminating trees, food plots, buildings, or other non-grassland habitat from within the patch can also reduce edge effects.

Predation is often more intense along the edges of a prairie because many predators that hunt in prairies live in nearby habitats. Examples include raccoons, foxes, bluejays, crows, and hawks. Those predators tend to hunt in areas close to their den or nest to conserve energy and time, which means that the animals living near the edges of prairies are more likely to get eaten. Predators also like to use edges as pathways for hunting, patrolling territories, and for traveling to and from other sites.

The term *microclimate* describes the temperature, wind, and humidity that occur in a small site (under a shrub, for example). On a summer day, the conditions under a shrub are likely to be slightly cooler, less windy, and more humid than in the grass a few feet away. Even that small difference in microclimate can have a big impact on plants and animals. Some species of plants are well adapted to the microclimate around shrubs but others are not, and many insects are very particular about temperature because of their need to regulate their body heat. So if a small prairie patch is surrounded by shrubs and trees, the outer edge of that prairie is less hospitable to plants and insects that need open grassland—making the patch effectively smaller for those species.

Invasive species often invade prairies from the edge, just as predators do. The more edge around a prairie, the better chance there is that an invader will find a way in. Many invasive species can also take advantage of the small microclimate differences between habitats on the edge and in the open prairie. For example, a prairie patch surrounded by shrubs would be much more likely to be invaded by eastern redcedars, Siberian elms, and other invasive trees and shrubs than a similarly sized prairie surrounded by cropland. Seeds from trees like eastern redcedar are spread by birds who eat their berries and drop the undigested seed to the ground. Normally they do this while perching in a tree or shrub—meaning that the portions of a prairie nearest trees are most likely to get seeded. Siberian elms and other trees that rely on the wind or other variable means to disperse their seeds drop most of their seeds close by, which means that the portion of a prairie nearest those trees will get most of that seed. The microclimate conditions near the edges of shrubs and trees are favorable to the growth of new shrubs and trees too, helping them to creep into prairies steadily, a little at a time.

Patch Layout and Connectivity

In addition to patch size and shape, the way patches are laid out across a landscape is also important (figure 7). The distance between prairie patches, corridors of grassland that might connect them, and the makeup of the landscape in between those prairies can all affect grassland species and communities. Prairies that are closer to each other are more likely to allow animals, seeds, and pollen to move between them. Corridors of grass, like grassy roadsides or cropland terraces, can provide pathways of movement between prairies for

Figure 7. Habitat patches in an imaginary landscape. Patches A and B are relatively large, but function as an even larger unit because they are connected by a corridor. Patch C is small but may be close enough to patch A that some species can move back and forth between them. Patch D is isolated but may be large enough to sustain populations of some species. Patch E is both small and isolated and is at high risk for losing species diversity over time.

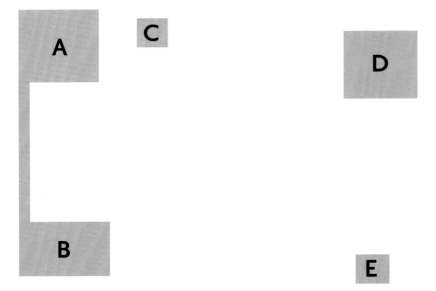

Plants with windblown seeds, such as this stiff goldenrod, can sometimes spread their progeny over long distances, but the vast majority of seeds land near the plant, so even these species can suffer from landscape fragmentation that separates prairies from each other.

some species that might otherwise be unable to leave their home patch. (Of course, those same corridors can also provide pathways for invasive species, so connectivity is not always a positive thing.)

Connectivity is most important when the landscape between prairies is completely inhospitable to prairie species that might want to travel through it. Some small mammals, for instance, might be more willing to travel through a wooded area full of hiding places than across a barren cropfield where they are exposed to hawks. On the other hand, a grasshopper might find a cornfield more accommodating than a woodlot where there's no recognizable food to eat. Some landscape features like rivers and highways can act as barriers to travel for animals like earthworms or ants, but are a minor inconvenience for butterflies and bees. Similarly, a single row of trees might not cause any problems for a migrating snake, but might catch most or all of the windblown seed and pollen from a prairie on one side, preventing it from getting to another prairie on the other side.

Being able to move (either themselves or their offspring) from one place to another is very important for the long-term survival of both plants and animals for several reasons. First, breeding with members of the same species with different genetic composition prevents inbreeding and keeps a species genetically diverse and ready to adapt to changing conditions. Second, the ability to move between patches allows a species to recolonize a patch where it has disappeared because of predation, disease, or other factors. This kind of connection between small populations in their local patches forms what biologists call a *metapopulation*. A metapopulation is comprised of a number of small local populations that interact with each other. Being part of a meta-population greatly increases the likelihood that a species in a small patch will survive because it can receive immigrants from populations in nearby patches.

As an example of the importance of metapopulations and the arrangement of patches across a landscape, let's take another look at our imaginary but-terfly population. The red-spotted flitters in the 10-acre prairie would be very unlikely to survive if that 10-acre prairie was isolated in a landscape full of cropfields and woodlots. One bad year could result in the loss of that species in the prairie forever. However, if there were other prairies nearby, the chance that other butterflies could find the 10-acre prairie would increase. That chance would increase even more if there were grassy roadsides or similar corridors connecting those prairies. And if those roadsides contained flowers to get nectar from or even false skunkweed plants to lay eggs on, it would be very likely that flitters would move back and forth between prairies. In that case, the flitters in the 10-acre population might actually be part of a meta-population of flitters spread over several hundred acres of prairie, and their long-term survival would be more secure.

prairie
management

Prescribed fire can be an important component of a prairie management regime. Like any management tool, however, it can be applied in various ways, each with different results.

This section of the book will incorporate

all of the factors that influence prairie community diversity, as presented pre-viously, into a set of management practices. More important, it will give you ideas on how to set good objectives, try a variety of strategies, evaluate your progress, and adjust strategies as needed. Following that process will be the most important thing you can do to ensure success.

Too many times, land managers find a technique or two that they are com-fortable with, and they simply employ that technique over and over. Unfor-tunately, there is no single management system that will fit the needs of your prairie, because your management will need to change as conditions change. Years of low or high moisture, encroachment by invasive species, and changes in populations of native herbivores such as deer—these are examples of con-ditions that can require you to adapt your strategies. Be flexible, remember your objectives, and identify the challenges you face. Then use what you know about how your prairie works, design strategies to address the challenges, and keep an eye on your prairie's response. When things aren't moving in the right direction, change your strategies.

The philosophy behind the management practices presented here is that good prairie management promotes biological diversity, not just enhanced habitat for one or two species. If you focus too narrowly on one component of the system, you can impair the complex interrelationships that define a prairie and keep it humming along. In other words, if you simplify your management, the prairie can become simplified as well. When that happens, you start to lose the natural processes that can give your prairie the resilience to bounce back from drought, repel invasive species, and otherwise respond to challenges it will certainly face. Conversely, if you manage for a diversity of native species and communities, everything in the prairie, including grassland birds, game species, butterflies, and wildflowers, will do well.

prairie management

Changing your strategy as conditions change is the most important component of a good prairie management regime. Adaptive management consists of 4 basic steps: setting objectives, taking action, measuring progress, and adjusting your objectives and strategies based on what you learn. Following an adaptive management process helps ensure that you will learn from your experiences and improve your prairie management over time.

Setting Objectives

The most critical part of the process is setting good objectives, because you can't measure progress if you don't know where you want to go. It might be helpful to start by developing a broad vision for what you want to accomplish on your property. Then devise 4 or 5 specific objectives that will move you in that direction. As you go along, your vision will probably not change much, but your objectives should change regularly as you make progress or as conditions change.

One vision or objective you should avoid is that of creating a "natural" or "historical" prairie. There are a couple of good reasons not to try to manage a prairie to fit some historical mold. First, prairies have been evolving for thousands of years, and choosing a snapshot in time to manage for would be like trying to keep your own appearance just as it was when you were 15. Second,

conditions have changed dramatically, even during the last 100 years. Aside from huge climate variations that have included long dry and wet periods, the increasing human development of prairie landscapes has brought a whole new set of variables, particularly habitat fragmentation and invasive species, that influence the look and function of prairies. A wise manager will learn about the historical conditions that drove the evolution of prairie species and their survival strategies, but that information must now be only a part of what drives management decisions.

Before setting your objectives, be sure to talk to local prairie experts and other prairie managers. Get a feel for what kinds of species diversity you might expect on your property, given the soil types, topography, size, and other factors. Are there rare plant or animal species that might use your site? If so, are there management options available to encourage them? What are the major invasive species in the area, and should you be setting objectives to eradicate them from your site, or is it more reasonable to attempt to keep them at some low level of abundance?

Setting objectives for the plant community will be your most important job, because the quality of the plant community influences all of the other biological diversity of the prairie. Think about both the total number of plant species across the site and the diversity of plants on a small scale. Generally speaking, a high-quality prairie can have a total of between 150 and 300 plant species. Higher numbers are usually found in larger prairies, prairies on richer soils, and prairies with more variety in topography and plant community types. However, remember that species diversity takes into account both the number of species *and* the frequency with which those species are found in the prairie. In other words, just because you can find 150 different plant species that show up at least once on your site doesn't necessarily mean that the prairie is in great shape—but it's a good start.

Looking at the density of species in your prairie is another good way to evaluate quality. In addition to having a plant species count across the whole site, a good prairie should also have a diverse mix of species on the scale of a square meter or so. This is a measure that many ecologists use for evaluating

This prescribed fire was conducted well into the spring season when invasive cool-season grasses were growing strongly. Noting the conditions that allowed the fire to burn well and revisiting the site to see whether or not the objectives were met are both components of good adaptive management.

prairies, so it's likely that there will be comparable information available from nearby prairies. An average count of between 15 and 20 species per square meter is very good in many prairies. However, in drier or more western prairies, that might be too ambitious, so talk to local experts to help you think about this. If this kind of measurement seems daunting, remember that you won't have to identify all the species you see, just look to see how many different species there are. The combination of good small-scale diversity and a total species count of 150–300 across the whole prairie is a pretty clear indication that your plant community is doing well. Lower small-scale diversity (fewer than 10 plant species per square meter) might mean that a few species are dominating the prairie at the expense of others.

Once you have objectives for the overall plant community, you can think about measuring the presence and abundance of rare, or conservative, species. A conservative species is one that is most often found in intact high-quality natural areas and doesn't usually survive chronic overgrazing, broadcast herbicide spraying, habitat fragmentation, or other such threats. If your prairie has a number of conservative plant species and they are reasonably abundant, it probably means that your prairie is in good shape. It can also mean that your prairie is contributing significantly to the diversity and function of the surrounding landscape, which may not contain many of those species. Depending upon the species, you may be able to do a simple count of individuals across the site (compass plants, for example). In other cases, it might be easier to pick out a couple of random portions of the prairie and monitor the number of individuals you see each year in that smaller area. Contact local conservation organizations to get a list of conservative plant and animal species for your area, and to get advice on how you might think about monitoring their abundance.

Setting objectives with regard to invasive species is critical. Some species, like invasive trees, can be easy to set objectives for: you can keep them out of the prairie altogether, keep them under a certain number of individuals, or restrict them to a certain number of acres or portion of the property. Other invasive species, like leafy spurge or Canada thistle, may occur in patches, and you can think about reducing the size of those patches and/or the number of those patches over time. With still other invasives, including grasses like

Some plant species, like wholeleaf rosinweed, can sometimes be all but eliminated from prairies under high levels of deer browsing. Increasing the abundance of rare plant species might be a management objective for your prairie.

smooth brome or Kentucky bluegrass, it can be very difficult to set good objectives for control because they tend to be almost ubiquitous in at least some parts of a prairie. In those cases, it might make more sense to simply rely on an objective about the average number of plant species per square meter, because the biggest threat from those invasives is that they can reduce diversity. If your plant diversity on a small scale remains high, you can usually feel confident that the invasives are not causing big problems.

Good objectives are both clear and measurable. You'll need to be thinking about how you plan to measure your progress toward an objective as you set it. In other words, if you're not planning to count plant species across your prairie, it won't do any good to set an objective in that regard. If you are planning weed control, figure out your strategy and set objectives that make sense based on that strategy.

An example of a poor objective would be this: "I would like to get rid of the Canada thistle in my prairie." A better objective might be, "I would like to reduce the number of Canada thistle patches from 20 to 5 within 4 years, and prevent the remaining patches from setting seed each year." That is a reasonable goal, and you can easily measure whether or not you're making progress. You may still be working toward the complete eradication of Canada thistle, but you can take it in steps, allowing yourself to measure effectiveness and progress and readjust strategies if you don't seem to be moving in the right direction. Below is a sampling of objectives for a hypothetical prairie. These are presented only as examples of how you might think about setting objectives. It's a good idea to keep the number of objectives to a handful at any time, so that you don't have too many things to keep track of. Remember that you'll change the objectives frequently as you take action and evaluate your progress.

Example Objectives
1. Maintain at least 140 native prairie plant species across the prairie.
2. Increase the average number of plant species per square meter from 10 to 12 within 4 years.
3. See at least 2 regal fritillary butterflies within one of three 100-by-10-yard transects each July for 3 consecutive years.
4. Find at least 5 singing Henslow's sparrow males in 2 out of the next 3 years.

5. Within the next 4 years, eliminate all eastern redcedar trees from the north half of the prairie and eliminate all the cedars with berries from the south half.
6. Reduce the number of autumn olive trees to no more than 3 per acre within 2 years, and eliminate any tree over 4 feet tall.
7. Within 3 years, eliminate all crownvetch patches less than 10 feet in diameter.

Taking Action

Once you have your objectives set, start working toward them. Spray the thistles, find a grazing lessee, and cut those trees out of the corner of the prairie. If you're doing something you've not tried before, it may be a good idea to do it in a way that makes it easy to evaluate whether it's working or not. For example, if you're trying to suppress Kentucky bluegrass with a late April fire, burn most of the area you want to affect, but leave a few small areas unburned. Then you can watch both treatments for a couple of years to see whether your fire actually made any difference. If you burn the entire site, you'll never know for sure whether any perceived suppression was because of your management or because it happened to be a bad year for bluegrass. Then you might waste valuable time and energy repeating the treatment several times before you realize that it's not really getting you anywhere. The more you can take action in ways that allow you to measure success, the faster you'll learn and the more effective your management will be. The remainder of this book deals with strategies and actions, so we'll skip past them for now.

Measuring Success

This is the step in which you evaluate whether or not your actions are helping you achieve your objectives. Take a step back and see if the Canada thistle is really decreasing because of your management. Is the Kentucky bluegrass giving way to a more diverse mix of native species? Are the trees you cut down dead, or are they resprouting? Evaluating the effectiveness of your strategies early on will help you manage more efficiently and not waste time and resources on actions that aren't working.

Measuring success can be as simple or complex as you want it to be. The most important thing is to make sure your evaluation feeds back to your objectives. If you set good objectives, your evaluation strategy should be pretty clear. If you are trying to eliminate eastern redcedars from the north half of the property, walk the north half and see if there are any left. If you are trying to decrease the number of autumn olive trees to fewer than 3 per acre, pick a couple of random acres and do a count.

For objectives that are more difficult to quantify, such as plant diversity on the square meter scale, it's good to get some input on techniques from local experts. You'll obviously have to match your evaluation strategies with the amount of time you have available and with your skill level. It might be a little overambitious to lay out 100 plots each year and count the number of plant species in each one. If so, don't write an objective that calls for that. Instead, consider other techniques that might provide similar information. For example, setting up 3–5 permanent plots (5–10 square meters in size) in random places around your prairie can allow you to measure changes over time in those same exact locations and see how your management is affecting the plant community. You can set objectives based on those plots, whether it is the total number of plant species you see, or the number of plants of a conservative or invasive species.

In addition to measuring progress toward your specific objectives, it's also good to evaluate the effectiveness of individual management treatments. As mentioned earlier, if you're using prescribed fire to reduce the abundance of Kentucky bluegrass, it can be very effective simply to leave unburned patches and see whether or not the fire has made a difference. However, even in very simple cases like that, it is useful to take notes of some kind on what you're seeing. One of the most powerful tools you can have as a prairie manager is a good field journal. In your journal you can record observations of management treatment effects, responses of your prairie to dry versus wet years, interesting species you see, and anything else you want. As the years go by, re-reading your notes from previous years can be extremely helpful as you try to see whether you're making progress toward your vision as well as to put the current year's observations in context.

If you do nothing else in terms of evaluation, set up some kind of photo monitoring system. If you have permanent plots set up, take photos of them each year, to accompany any data you collect. If you don't have permanent

A plot frame can be useful to measure the density or abundance of plants across your prairie, but it is not the only way to accomplish that.

plots, set up several points from which you can take the same photo at the same time every year. If you've got a thistle problem you're trying to control, you might take an annual photo during peak thistle bloom. Otherwise, just pick a date in the middle of the summer, or several dates, and photograph from the same place and at the same angle each time. The combination of a good field journal and annual photo points can provide a lot of information to guide your management.

Adjusting Your Strategies and Objectives

Once you've measured the effectiveness of your work, it's critical to use that information to adjust your strategies and objectives. If you've burned your bluegrass three years in a row and haven't seen much of a decrease in abundance, it's probably time to try something else. If you try several different strategies and still aren't seeing a decrease, it might be time to change the objective. Can you increase forb diversity or habitat structure regardless of whether or not the bluegrass is still there? Maybe you didn't change your bluegrass abundance much, but saw a big decrease in the Siberian elm stand in the same patch. Can you figure out why that happened and apply that knowledge to the bigger patch on the other half of the prairie? If so, you'll achieve at least some of your objectives, and you can scratch them off the list and write new, even more ambitious ones.

Using the adaptive management approach to set objectives, take action, measure progress, and adjust your strategies is extremely important. Remember that a single season, or sometimes even two or three, may not be enough to judge whether you're really making progress or not. The weather in a particular year can have a stronger effect on your objectives than your strategies, or it can make a strategy more or less effective than it would be in another year. In addition, many prairie plants can live for decades, so it can be hard to see changes in plant communities within a few years, even if many plants aren't reproducing successfully. Look at multiyear trends as much as you can, and try to learn from what others are doing too. Talk to your neighbors, local conservation biologists, and university professors. Learn what other people are trying and how it's working, and share what you're learning with them. Prairie management is still a relatively young field. Grasslands have long been managed for cattle and hay production, and there is a wealth of information on those subjects, but we still have a lot to learn about managing grasslands for biodiversity. The more we all experiment and share what we learn, the faster we'll build our understanding of these complex natural systems and how to maintain them.

7. Guiding Principles for Designing Management Strategies

As you design management strategies for your prairie, there are two principles that should guide you. First, managing a prairie really means managing
the competition between plants. All management strategies are designed to
manipulate plant competition in a way that pushes the plant community in a
desired direction. The second guiding principle is that diverse prairies require
diverse management treatments. Manipulating plant competition to favor
plant diversity takes a variety of tools, and you will need to vary the intensity
and frequency with which you use those tools.

One mistake commonly made by prairie managers is that they form a mental picture of what they think their prairie should look like—and then try
to make it look that way each year. This could be called the Calendar Prairie
Syndrome, in which a prairie manager wants his or her prairie to look like the
July landscape photo from a beautiful calendar. One of the best things about
prairies is their variability. Being able to see something different each time
you visit a prairie is a better goal than trying to make it look always the same.
If you aim for the calendar look, it's easy to fall into the trap of managing the
same way each year, and eventually diversity will suffer—as will some of the
big showy flowers that you're trying to manage for.

Prairies are always changing, in part because their plants are in constant
competition with each other. Your job is to recognize and understand the

competition and to manipulate it so that each species wins often enough to stay in the community. Most of that manipulation will occur through a variety of methods of defoliating plants. Defoliation isn't always pretty. In fact, both individual plants and prairies as a whole can look pretty ragged when they've been chewed on by cattle, mowed off, or reduced to ashes by a fire. But in many ways, the true beauty of prairies is their ability to respond to those kinds of events. That ability to respond helps them to maintain their diversity and integrity and to repel trees and other invasive species.

Manage the vigor of your prairie as you would manage your own physical fitness. Stress different components of the prairie at different times and intensities, and use a variety of tools to accomplish that. Mix rest periods in between periods of stress. Making sure that every component of a prairie is in good shape will allow it to respond most effectively to stress, including the disturbances you use for management.

Manipulating Competition

Plants are constantly competing with each other for water, nutrients, light, and space. Those plants that compete best in a particular soil type, during a particular weather cycle, or under a particular disturbance regime increase their abundance while the losers begin to fade. Your job as a prairie manager is to manipulate the system. It's like helping your kid's team win a game—without the ethical implications—except that with prairies, you are constantly changing the teams (species) you favor so that they all get to win now and then. In that way, the entire diversity of desirable plants is sustained in your prairie.

There are several ways to influence plant competition. The first is by directly killing the plants that are competing against the ones you're favoring. In prairie management, this approach is appropriate when you're trying to eliminate invasive species that are outcompeting native plants. The second way is to manipulate the playing conditions to favor the strengths of the species you're trying to help. A prescribed fire is a good example of this. Burning a prairie removes litter and helps plants grow faster because of the additional light hitting the ground. Some plants, particularly grasses, will respond more quickly

Be careful not to form a mental photograph of what you want your prairie to look like. Healthy prairie communities change in appearance from year to year as well as from season to season, in response to varying environmental conditions and management strategies.

Blackeyed Susan is one of many short-lived prairie plants whose continued presence in a prairie depends upon frequent establishment of new seedlings.

to that opportunity than others. By setting the ground rules, you help decide who will win. The third and most important way you can influence competition is by weakening some plants to allow others to gain an advantage. When a plant is partially or completely defoliated (when it has its leaves or stems cut, bitten, burned, or torn off) it can't compete as strongly for space and resources. Most prairie management treatments are essentially methods of defoliating plants.

The Impact of Defoliation on Plants

In the first section of this book, the general impacts of fire and grazing on plant communities were presented. Much of the specific impact of those disturbances comes from defoliation. While fire and grazing are the major natural forms of defoliation, mowing and haying can also remove leaves and stems. Defoliation weakens a plant because it decreases its capacity to photo-

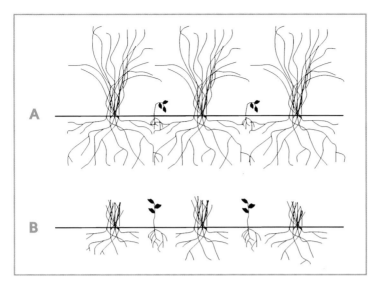

Figure 8. Generalized aboveground and belowground responses of plants to defoliation. Example A shows dominant grasses at full strength. There is no root space or available light for new seedlings of other species to establish between grass plants. In example B, the grass plants have been severely defoliated and are unable to support more than a small root area. This provides root space and light for new species to germinate and establish themselves successfully in the plant community.

synthesize, or to turn sunlight into energy. It also forces the plant to regrow the parts that were removed, using energy the plant would have otherwise devoted to root growth or reproduction. A weakened plant can't maintain the same root system that a strong plant can, so when a plant is severely or repeatedly defoliated, it has to abandon parts of its root system. This usually means that the roots become shorter and the total area covered by the plant's root system becomes smaller. In combination with the increased light available above ground because of the defoliation of the plant, this smaller root zone opens up space for other plants to establish or expand (figure 8).

For example, if big bluestem were being targeted for intensive grazing by cattle in a particular prairie, all of those big bluestem plants would lose root mass and most of their leaves. This would allow more light to hit the ground and the surrounding plants, encouraging them to grow more strongly and/or encouraging seeds to germinate. At the same time, the smaller area covered

by the big bluestem roots below ground opens up space and available moisture for the new or expanding plants. If you allow defoliation of big bluestem to continue in the same way for many years, it will gradually become less dominant across the prairie as other species take over the aboveground and belowground territory left open by weakened bluestem plants.

The way a plant responds after a defoliation event depends on its life strategy, the moisture available, and the timing of the defoliation. Perennial plants tend to have stronger and more resilient root systems to fuel recovery than do annual or biennial plants. However, perennials can also afford not to put energy into reproduction during a particularly tough year. If you repeatedly defoliate a perennial for most of the growing season, it is likely simply to enter dormancy early and skip flowering or rhizome production. An annual or biennial plant, though, has fewer options because it gets only one chance to bloom and reproduce. Annuals, in particular, will always bloom and produce seeds if they have any energy left to do so, though defoliated annuals will often produce fewer and smaller flowers than they would otherwise have done. Some biennials may be able to skip flowering in one particular year and try again the next, but they have a limited number of opportunities because of their short lifespan.

Available moisture also contributes to the way a plant responds. Severely defoliated plants are more likely to go dormant under drought conditions than when moisture is available to help with regrowth. If defoliation occurs in dry weather, some plants may enter dormancy for the remainder of the year even if good rains come later in the season. Others may stop growing for a time, but resume growth and even flower later in the season if moisture returns.

The third factor influencing the response of plants to defoliation is the time of year and how it relates to the growth cycle of the particular species. Most prairie plants are most vulnerable to defoliation right as they're starting to bloom. At that point in their season, they have expended a great deal of energy in leaf and stem production, and they are putting even more energy into making flowers. Once the plant produces seeds, it starts sending energy back into its roots to prepare for dormancy (or, if it's an annual or biennial, it

Defoliation, by cattle or other means, is an important regulator of competition between plants. As one plant becomes weakened by defoliation, other plants take advantage by expanding their territories.

simply dies). But prior to that, it is putting the bulk of the energy it produces into growth. For that reason, grazing a plant to the ground right before bloom has the maximum impact on its regrowth potential. In contrast, defoliating most plants during their dormant season (when the plants are brown) has little impact on their regrowth, because grasses and forbs start each year's growth from ground level. Dormant prairie plants have their energy stored in their roots, and the only effect of dormant-season defoliation is that it might increase light availability and decrease soil moisture by removing the standing dead vegetation. Whether your objectives call for big or small impacts on particular plant species, your management decisions will be more effective if you understand how plants are likely to respond to your treatments.

The Impact of Drought on Plants

Besides defoliation, plants have to respond to other kinds of disturbances as well. Chief among these is drought. The combination of extreme heat and low moisture, especially over extended periods, can affect plants in ways somewhat similar to defoliation. The lack of available moisture limits the size and number of leaves a plant can produce, and that limits the amount of energy the plant can produce to support its root system. So dry conditions limit both the aboveground and belowground size of a plant. And, as mentioned above, drought can intensify the impact of defoliation and diminish its ability to respond.

Of course, the root architecture of different plant species affects their ability to use moisture under stress. Plants with deep taproots may be able to reach groundwater or deeper soil moisture during drought than can shallow-rooted plants. This can be a great advantage during long droughts, but it has disadvantages too. When it does rain, most of the water will not get far down into the soil before it gets picked up by those shallow-rooted plants. So if a plant has invested most of its root energy into growing deep roots, it may miss out on short-term bursts of moisture.

While you can't control drought, you do need to understand its impact on plants so that you can adjust your management accordingly. Prescribed fires, grazing, haying, and other management treatments that defoliate plants will all have a more severe impact under drought conditions. It's difficult to pre-

Drought can be an important regulator of plant vigor, particularly in western prairies where extended dry periods are frequent. Plants that are dominant during wet periods may become much less abundant during droughts (and vice versa).

dict drought ahead of time, especially in localized areas, but you can adjust your management during or following droughts.

Diverse Management Treatments

The second guiding principle when managing for plant diversity is that you need to allow every native plant species to reproduce and sustain itself in the prairie community. This means that your management has to favor the growth and reproduction of each species periodically so that it doesn't get pushed out of the community. Imagine that you're planning a party for a diverse group of people and you have to choose the games that will be played. You probably wouldn't choose only physically demanding games like arm wrestling and tackle football. Similarly, you wouldn't choose only games like

Scrabble or bridge that require a certain level of experience and education. In either case, only a subset of your friends would enjoy themselves because the others wouldn't ever stand a chance of winning. You might get away with it for a while, but if you kept playing the same games for too long the people who kept losing would probably leave the party. If you kept playing the same games every time you hosted a party, you'd eventually end up with a much smaller group of guests.

Applying that idea to prairie management, if you manage for occupier plants for a year or two, be sure to manage for colonizers the next year. Or, if the prairie is large enough, you might manage for occupiers in one part and colonizers in another and then switch the next year. Of course that's very simplistic, and it addresses only a single aspect of one part of the prairie community, the reproductive strategy of plants. At the same time you're doing that, you'd also want to consider whether you're favoring warm-season or cool-season plants, the impact of your management on the balance between grasses and forbs, and whether or not invasive species are gaining or losing ground.

Managing a prairie so that everybody gets to win now and then means that you have to use treatments that vary across time and space. Because we can't control climate, the two major disturbances left to us are fire and grazing (and substitutes such as mowing). Varying the timing, frequency, and intensity of those treatments is the mechanism by which you can introduce heterogeneity and diversity. For example, you might use an early spring fire one year, rest the prairie for a year or two, and then conduct a late spring or summer fire next. Grazing is even more flexible because you can control the timing (when and for how long cattle are on the prairie), frequency (how often you put cattle in), and intensity (number of animals in a given area).

Avoiding Repetition

Health experts emphasize variety in exercise regimens in order to keep your body in top shape. Not only should you exercise, but you should vary the type and intensity of exercise (and include rest periods) to prevent your body from adapting to a particular pattern. That's an excellent metaphor for prairie management. A healthy, well-managed body can resist disease and perform a wide

While prescribed fire can be an excellent management tool, the repetitive use of fire can also limit the diversity of prairie plants unless its timing and frequency are varied.

variety of activities well. A healthy, well-managed prairie can resist invasive species and support a wide variety of plants and animals.

Homogeneous management (doing the same thing over and over) leads to homogeneous prairies. The obvious examples of this are grasslands that are either hayed every year at the same time or grazed each year in exactly the same way. Prairies that are hayed each year in the middle of summer, for example, can develop a distinctive look, characterized by abundant cool-season grasses (particularly nonnative species), weak stands of warm-season grasses, and a lack of late-blooming forbs. They also tend to have a very monotonous vegetation structure, both horizontally and vertically (although there are notable examples of hayed prairies that have maintained a diverse plant community over many years—see the next chapter's discussion on haying). Repetitively grazed pastures, especially if they are grazed intensively for the entire season, year after year, tend to become dominated by those plant species that cattle prefer not to eat—Kentucky bluegrass, ragweeds, hoary vervain, goldenrods, for example. Either way, these prairies lack plant diversity because the management system consistently favors some plants over others. Those that are not favored can fade slowly out of the community.

To prevent repetition, it's important to use a diversity of tools and management strategies. It's also important to keep a plant community from conforming itself to a particular pattern of management over time. Even rotational grazing or burning systems can lead to losses in plant diversity. For example, burning a site every third spring (or burning a third each year) leads to a plant community adapted to that regimen. In some prairies, this is expressed by an abundance of shrubs like smooth sumac and an overabundance of grasses relative to forbs. Rotational grazing can be beneficial for plant communities, but not if the pattern remains the same over time. Altering the length of time between fires or grazing periods, periodically changing the intensity of grazing, and varying the season in which fire or grazing is applied can all help to prevent patterns from becoming established.

It is especially important to vary management regimes on prairies that grow in soils with high levels of organic matter and that receive reliable moisture. Prairies with consistent growing conditions are at a higher risk of losing plant diversity to repetitive management than those with less-consistent conditions. For example, a prairie growing in rich soil and in an area with relatively predictable rainfall during the summer is likely to look very much the same each year under similar management conditions. In contrast, a prairie on sandy or rocky soils, especially in the western part of the Midwest where rainfall is sporadic within and between seasons, is likely to look very different from year to year because it is responding to those variable conditions—even if it's managed the same way. Variable growing conditions can help maintain diversity because some plants do better than others in some years and worse in others, and it's difficult for any species to become completely dominant at the expense of others. Imposing variable growing conditions through management can help keep plants on their toes and level the playing field for a greater number of species.

There are numerous tools and strategies available for managing prairies, including prescribed fire, grazing, mowing, haying, herbicide application, and rest. When trying to promote biodiversity, you should consider using a variety of these strategies. Following are several generalized examples of management systems. They include examples of systems without cattle and/ or fire, but, when feasible, the combination of fire and grazing can be a key component of a diversity-friendly management regime. If both fire and grazing are available to you, you should still read the other examples, because they are written to provide cumulative advice. In other words, management strategies that don't require fire and grazing can still be used to complement or supplement a fire/grazing system. These examples will not cover some issues, such as invasive-species challenges, in detail. However, invasive species will be dealt with in the next chapter, and strategies to deal with them can be incorporated into most of these systems.

Management without Fire or Cattle

If neither fire nor grazing is feasible at your site, find other ways to simulate the desired impact of those disturbances. Mowing and/or haying can be used to defoliate growing plants and to prevent an excess buildup of thatch from suppressing plant growth. The difference between mowing and haying is that haying involves the removal of the cut material. In many cases, haying is preferable since thick swaths of cut hay lying on the prairie can kill the vegetation underneath them. If you do mow, doing it when the prairie vegetation is still fairly short can reduce the possibility of smothering plants under excessive litter. Raising the mower deck and cutting higher can do the same thing.

Because it removes the cut vegetation from the site and doesn't allow it to decompose, repeated haying can slowly diminish the nutrient content of the soil, especially the phosphorus, potash, and nitrogen, with mixed results. Loss of nutrients can reduce productivity, but lower levels of nitrogen, in particular, can help increase plant diversity by favoring forbs over grasses. Extra nitrogen from years of fertilization or deposition from nearby agricultural fields can assist the invasion of exotic cool-season grasses. In Europe, biologists are finding that multiple decades of annual haying can actually improve plant diversity by reducing nitrogen levels that favor a few dominant plants. In North America there are prairies that have been hayed annually for years and have maintained a strong and diverse plant community. This is especially true for prairies that are hayed late in the season, after most plants have had an opportunity to flower. However, annual haying can also have a number of disadvantages, especially if cutting is done at the same time each year.

One big disadvantage of haying (and mowing) in a diversity-friendly management system is that it is nonselective. Every plant species is cut to the same height when the mower comes past, as opposed to the selective grazing done by cattle or other grazers. Just as clear-cutting does in a forest, haying homogenizes the vegetation structure of the community, and repeated haying can sometimes reduce plant diversity. You can help mitigate this in a prairie by taking advantage of the fact that plants grow and bloom at different times of the year. For example, mowing the prairie in early June will have a strong impact on the vigor of cool-season grasses and early-season forbs that are just preparing to bloom. They will have expended a great deal of energy preparing for flowering and will lose all that energy when they are mowed off. By contrast, most warm-season grasses and late-season flowering forbs will just be getting started, and will easily recover from an early-season mowing. Likewise, mowing in August will have little impact on plants that have already flowered and become dormant for the year, but will affect severely those

Haying can be part of a successful management strategy for a diverse prairie community, but it is a nonselective treatment, creating homogeneous vegetation structure.

just preparing to flower. Cutting hay in the late summer can also favor cool-season grasses (including many invasive species) by increasing the amount of sunlight available during their fall and spring growth periods. Mowing during the dormant season (November through March) can remove thatch and standing dead vegetation from the prairie without having any immediate impact on plant vigor (except for that of shrubs and trees). In addition, as most prairie plants enter dormancy, they return many nutrients from their leaves and stems to their roots. Haying or mowing the prairie in the dormant season, then, reduces the amount of nutrient loss that might take place if the prairie is mowed when the vegetation is still green. In summary, haying in any season will benefit some plant species over others, but varying the timing from year to year can help to prevent any group of plants from becoming too strong or too weak over time.

Another disadvantage of haying and mowing is that both can be destructive to wildlife. This is especially true when haying takes place in the middle of nesting season or even when birds are recently fledged. Haying equipment can kill or injure birds directly, of course, and the immediate and dramatic change in habitat structure can greatly affect the survival of many wildlife species. This means that there are often conflicts between wildlife and plant community considerations in the timing of haying operations. As discussed above, haying in early June or when cool-season grasses are preparing to flower can be important for affecting the balance between cool-season and warm-season plants. Unfortunately, that is also the peak nesting period for most grassland birds and a critical time for many other wildlife species that are trying to hide nests, dens, and young from predators. Similarly, mid July is about the time haying can have the strongest impact on warm-season grass dominance, opening opportunities for increased forb diversity. However, it's also when young grassland birds are just learning to fly and are particularly vulnerable to predation—especially when their protective vegetation cover is suddenly removed. With a more selective and gradual defoliation method like grazing, all of the above wildlife damage issues can be greatly mitigated.

As you have probably guessed, a diversity-friendly system that relies only on mowing and haying will need to incorporate a variety of the aforementioned timing options. It is important to periodically reduce the vigor of existing plants to allow new plants to become established between them. The key is to alter which species are affected from year to year and to avoid falling into a set pattern. In addition to varying the frequency and season of mowing or haying, varying the height at which the vegetation is cut may be beneficial. Mowing vegetation to a height of 6–8 inches (or more) will allow a much faster recovery than mowing down to the ground, because the plants will still have a number of leaves to help fuel their regrowth. Sometimes fast recovery is useful, particularly if there are concerns with soil erosion or invasive species that might take advantage of bare ground. In other situations, a slower recovery can allow more space for new seedlings to grow and become established before the mature plants reestablish their dominance.

In terms of habitat for wildlife species, mowing and haying do not generally provide very good habitat-structure heterogeneity. At any one time, the prairie is either short or tall, with very little middle ground or patchiness. However, there is nothing that prevents you from mowing patches, strips, or random paths through the prairie. While it doesn't provide the kind of selective defoliation that grazing does, patch-mowing can provide better habitat than uniformly short or tall vegetation. It also prevents a number of potential problems for wildlife species that can result from completely uniform defoliation of a prairie—particularly one that is isolated from other grasslands. For example, strip-mowing provides refuges for insects and wildlife species that need tall cover to survive during either the summer or winter, or both. It also maintains a steady availability of food for pollinators and other insects throughout the entire growing season. On a cautionary note, if one of your objectives is to support diverse populations of grassland birds, it might be important to maintain some relatively large areas (10–25 acres) of fairly consistent vegetation structure, if possible, to provide appropriate nesting habitat and territory size. Birds that require short vegetation structure for nesting may not gain much from the presence of thin strips of short grass through an otherwise tall prairie. In addition, as mentioned earlier, haying between May and August can be hard on nesting birds and other wildlife species. You will have to find your own balance between the long-term benefits to the prairie and the short-term impact on wildlife. Just remember that if the prairie suffers a long-term decline in quality, its wildlife will too.

One advantage of haying over mowing is that you can derive some income from the property. However, varied haying techniques produce varied hay quality as well. If you are haying the property yourself, it's relatively easy to convince yourself to cut at varying times of year and at varying frequencies, as long as you aren't doing it for maximum profit. If someone else is haying the property for you, it can be a challenge to convince him or her to cut hay in August after several years of growth (hard on machinery and low-quality hay), to cut the vegetation 6–8 inches off the ground (less quantity and difficult for some kinds of hay equipment), or to cut in May (less quantity and in the middle of rowcrop planting season). Some concessions may have to be made to logistics (or the lease rate reduced) in order to find someone willing to follow a somewhat unorthodox haying schedule.

In addition to mowing or haying, another strategy that can be employed is light disking or harrowing. The objectives of this kind of treatment are to expose areas of bare soil to improve the chances for seed germination, and to weaken the root structure (and therefore the vigor) of the dominant prairie plants to help new seedlings survive. As with mowing treatments, disking and harrowing can be applied in patches or strips, and there are ways to vary the intensity of the disturbance. Disking with the disk blades straight (pointing the same direction as the disk is being pulled) versus angled reduces the amount of soil that is turned over, but still cuts through roots of plants to reduce vigor. Deep versus shallow disking and harrowing, with or without weight on top of the harrow, can also provide varying degrees of soil disturbance. The purpose of treatments like this is not to turn the prairie into a cultivated field, but to shake up a plant community becoming dominated by a few species with little or no recruitment of new plants and species. The severity of the disturbance can be correlated with the perceived need, and small areas should serve as test sites to evaluate whether or not the treatment does what you want it to. In general, disking and harrowing should be seen as options to be used only on the rare occasions when no other option is available. It is very important to understand that any management that produces bare soil will likely increase the germination and establishment of both desired plants and invasive species. If you have invasive species that could become a much bigger problem with a sudden increase in bare ground, disking is probably not the best option, or it should be done in small areas where the invasives can be treated easily. If the disking is too aggressive, it can be counterproductive by killing plants that might not reestablish well, thus lowering plant diversity. In addition, disking can pose a great risk to some animals (particularly reptiles) that may not be able to get out of the way quickly enough.

When haying or mowing is the primary management tool being employed, it is important to consider what areas to cut from year to year. In general, management units should be overlapped between years. In other words, if a treatment (like haying) is split between the east and west halves one year, it can be split north/south or northeast/southwest, etc., the next year to help increase heterogeneity and reduce the possibility of developing permanent

Crownvetch is an example of an invasive plant that can take advantage of annual haying or mowing. Repetitive use of any management tool will favor some plants over others, eventually reducing plant diversity.

boundaries between management treatments. Those boundaries are often the places where invasive species, particularly woody plants, gain a foothold. Trees can be especially devious in this regard. For example, if you hay the north half of the prairie one year and the south half the next, it's likely that there will occasionally be a strip between the two units that doesn't get hayed with either the north or south unit. That can be just enough time for a couple of trees to establish and grow enough that, the next time the equipment comes past, the operator goes around them to avoid damage to the mower. Over time those trees will continue to grow and reproduce and eventually form a small grove or strip. Each year, the hay operator will mow around the strip, but the strip will tend to get larger and larger because the operator always leaves a small cushion between the machinery and the strip to avoid hitting trees. That cushion provides an area of continued expansion for the trees, and the grove continues to grow.

Finally, if you begin to alter the frequency of cutting on a prairie that has been perennially hayed, there may be plants that have been long suppressed but have survived years of repetitive defoliation. Some of those plants, including long-lived rare plants that greatly benefit plant diversity on the site, can be pleasant surprises. But oftentimes you will find that there are trees and shrubs that have endured annual defoliation but have managed to maintain or even increase their root mass underground. A year or two of no haying can release those woody plants, and their growth rate can be an unpleasant surprise. Be prepared for this by looking carefully for very short trees and shrubs before resting an entire hayed prairie. If there are numerous trees present, you may want to begin your new management by resting only small portions of the prairie at a time so that you can kill the trees in manageable numbers.

As mentioned earlier, some prairies can withstand annual haying for many years and retain excellent diversity. This may be related to season of haying, soil type, moisture, and a number of other factors. If you have a prairie that has been hayed for many years, it is not automatically necessary for you to change that, especially without talking to some local experts about the condition of your prairie. However, even if the prairie seems to have good plant diversity, there are some things to consider. First, is the diversity of plants in the community stable, or slowly declining? Because many plants can live for decades, some may survive annual cutting even if they are not allowed to flower and/or reproduce for many years. At some point, however, they may disappear from the system, and it may be difficult to predict when or whether that might happen. Second, be sure to investigate whether or not there are invasive species taking advantage of the repetitive haying. As mentioned above, many tree species can gain a foothold in a hayed prairie but not be very obvious because they are repeatedly mowed. In some situations, those trees and/or shrubs could become a problem, either by making haying more difficult because of their increased thickness or by getting abundant enough to begin outcompeting other plants. In addition to trees, many other invasive species can take advantage of repeated haying in the summer. These include cool-season grasses like smooth brome, tall fescue, and others, and other species like crownvetch. It can be difficult to tell whether these species are present in low but stable populations, or increasing a little each year. And in many instances the invasion starts out small and slow, but grows exponentially, gaining in size and rate of spread each year.

Management with Fire but without Cattle

If fire is an option, but cattle are not, all of the above techniques and ideas for haying and mowing can be combined with prescribed fire to provide a more diverse management system. The principles that apply to haying and mowing, in terms of variations in timing, frequency, and location, also apply to fire. Although fire is an important tool, and one that prairies respond well to, it's important to use it in a nonrepetitive fashion for all the same reasons already discussed.

Many of the effects of defoliation through mowing also apply to defoliation through fire. However, there are some important differences. One is the way fire affects the nutrient cycle of a prairie. Carbon and nitrogen are both lost from the prairie during a fire (they literally go up in smoke) but phosphorus is returned to the soil in the form of ash. There is often a noticeable increase in overall vegetative growth following a fire in a prairie. Most of that increase is probably due to nitrogen that built up in the soil during previous seasons without fire. During years of no fire (assuming no grazing or haying took place), increasing thatch and standing dead vegetation reduce the ability of plants to maximize growth. Because of that, roots shorten, leaving untapped nitrogen in portions of the soil. After a fire, plants take advantage of the increased light availability, and extend their roots into that untapped nitrogen, further increasing their rate of growth. Some scientists have speculated that increased growth is also aided by cyanobacteria stimulated by the phosphorus from the ash. Those cyanobacteria fix nitrogen in the soil, making it more available for plants to use.

Another difference between fire and haying is the amount of litter left on the soil surface. Most prescribed prairie fires burn all the vegetation completely, exposing bare soil with few stems or leaves remaining. This bare soil, combined with the dark color of the ash and soot, helps warm the soil in the spring and can speed up the emergence of plants. The top layer of the same bare soil can also dry out more than it would with haying, which can compound the effects of a drought or diminish the effects of a wet period. Of course, the magnitude of drying depends on when the fire takes place. A few weeks of drying soil in the spring, following an April fire, may have much less impact than an entire winter of bare ground following a November fire.

Another impact of fire is that it can help with seed germination of many plant species. Research has shown higher seed germination rates and germination of more plant species after a fire than under haying or mowing treatments. Some of this occurs because of the additional light hitting seeds on the ground. However, some plant species simply have much higher germination rates following fires because either the smoke or the heat helps to stimulate germination.

As mentioned earlier, fires can slow the spread of trees and shrubs into a prairie, although it is more effective on some species than others. An additional benefit of fire over mowing or haying is that it can be used in situations where trees or shrubs have become established to the point that mowing equipment cannot be used. While you can find brushcutting mowers that will cut through pretty large trunks, they can be expensive and are not feasible for everyone. On the other hand, prescribed fire can be used in an area with established trees and shrubs and can remove thatch, topkill (at least) the woody plants, and help clean out the debris so that mowing or haying can be used in the future.

Prescribed fires can be conducted at any time of year, including summertime, if adequate fuel (dried grass) is present. While this prairie was full of tall green vegetation, it had been rested the year before, and the dried grass from that growing season carried a summer fire easily.

Because of the differences between the effects of fire and of haying, there are a few things you should consider as you think about how to use fire effectively. Varying the timing, frequency, and location of fires is important, just as it is with haying or mowing. However, while it is possible to conduct a prescribed fire that burns everything to the ground, it is also possible to vary the intensity of the fire to some degree. The most important factor limiting the amount of vegetation that will be consumed by a fire is moisture. Burning when relative humidity is high reduces the intensity of the fire and can prevent it from burning anything other than the most flammable dry vegetation. High fuel moisture (the moisture of the vegetation being burned) can prevent grass or other plants from burning at all. Fires during the growing season are carried by the dry dead vegetation (the part that will actually burn). Even in the middle of the summer, fires can carry through a prairie if there is enough built-up thatch and dead vegetation to fuel them. However, growing-season fires are more likely to result in a patchwork of burned and unburned areas, particularly when thatch and litter are not superabundant. Areas with mostly green vegetation at the time of the fire will burn less completely, or not at all, than areas with mostly dead vegetation.

Another way to vary fire intensity is by the lighting technique used. A fire running with the wind at its back (a head fire) will have the highest and longest flames. This is the fastest type of fire and is the most effective at consuming fuels that are patchy or light. It can also be the most effective at killing eastern redcedar trees that are a little on the tall side because the higher flame heights can reach more of the trees. Sometimes, however, there may be cases where there are trees (e.g., scattered oak trees) that you would rather not kill. In those cases, a fire that backs into the wind (backing fire) or that is lit sideways to the wind (flank fire) might be safer. A backing fire will have lower flame heights, reducing the chance that flames or heat will reach the canopy of large trees. However, a backing fire also moves more slowly, which means that the heat may stay in any one place for a longer time. There is some belief that this can result in higher mortality of young trees because the small trunks may be "cooked" in a slow fire. To summarize, a head fire runs faster, will more completely consume patchier grass fuel, and can be more effective at topkilling large trees. A backing fire moves more slowly and will be less effective at completely consuming patchy fuels, but may create a more intense heat to consume woody fuels close to the ground. The right technique will depend upon your objectives for the fire.

Another thing to consider is that fires can sometimes help to strengthen plant species that are already too dominant in a community. For example, a late spring fire may temporarily suppress cool-season nonnative grasses like smooth brome but greatly enhance the growth of warm-season grasses like big bluestem—at the expense of many forb species. Historically, fires would have often attracted bison and other grazers, thereby moderating the growth of major grasses. However, in the absence of grazing, repeated late spring fires can lead to increased dominance of warm-season grasses and reduced overall plant diversity. Similarly, early spring or late summer fires can some-times help cool-season grasses exert dominance over warm-season grasses. Of course, all of these results may vary by geographic location, soil type, and the weather following the fire, and no two fires (or the prairie's responses to them) are ever exactly alike.

One way to keep grasses from becoming too dominant after a fire is to fol-low the fire with a mowing or haying treatment to reduce the vigor of the re-sponding vegetation. A late April fire followed by mowing in mid June or July, for example, might provide many benefits of the fire while somewhat sup-pressing the growth of grasses afterward. While this isn't always necessary, it may also help the survival of any new seedlings that appear after the fire by reducing competition from their quickly growing neighbors, especially if the vegetation is cut at a height of 6–8 inches or more.

Besides the potential to favor already dominant plants, fires can pose other threats to biodiversity as well. Most prairie wildlife is able to escape most fires, but there can be rare exceptions. A slower fire can help animals to es-cape, and burning when temperatures are relatively warm will allow snakes and other reptiles to move into burrows or other safe places. In addition, leav-ing some areas unburned can provide refuges for those animals that depend on dense vegetation for protective cover. Also, if it still meets your objectives, burning in the dormant season when vulnerable animals are hibernating can be beneficial.

Some insects are particularly vulnerable to fire, especially when they are in their egg or larval stage. Many insect species spend the winter as eggs or larvae and embed themselves in standing vegetation or within the litter above the ground. Because of this, one fire could potentially destroy all the individuals of an insect species within the burned area. Historically, prairies were large and fires burned only a portion of the total landscape each year, so insect species eradicated locally by a fire were able to move back in from near-by unburned areas. In the fragmented prairie landscape we have today, it's possible to completely eliminate an insect species (or multiple species) from a prairie by burning the entire prairie. If there is no unburned prairie nearby, that insect species may not have a way to return. Species that do not travel well (leafhoppers, for example) are especially susceptible to this because they

EXAMPLES OF MANAGEMENT SYSTEMS

may be unable to cross even small barriers like roads. If you are managing a prairie that is not well connected to other prairies with similar plant species, it's very important not to burn the entire prairie in the same year. Because of the importance of the relationships between insects and plants, losing an insect species might have a much greater impact on your prairie than just the loss of that single species.

In general, though, prairies are better off with fire than without. Despite the destructive nature of fire, prairies and prairie species have had thousands of years to become adapted to it. Fire can be more effective than other treatments at accomplishing some objectives, such as suppressing eastern red-cedars and some other tree species. It can also be helpful when you want to remove litter and stimulate seed germination and/or grass growth. However, it is a mistake to assume that fire will always be helpful just because it is a historical process. As with any other management tool, repetitive or nonjudicious use of fire can be counterproductive. In addition, fire can be dangerous, not only to prairie inhabitants but to humans and human belongings. Prescribed fire should be used only when it meets specific objectives and can be done safely and in accordance with local laws and guidelines.

Safely and effectively using prescribed fire as a management tool requires careful planning and a good deal of experience. Information on the mechanics of conducting a prescribed fire, and guidance on where and how to get training and equipment, are available in the appendix.

Management with Cattle but without Fire

Among prairie enthusiasts, cattle tend to have a bad reputation. This is understandable when you consider that many cattle pastures, particularly in more eastern landscapes, look like putting greens or at least have very few conservative prairie plants. It doesn't have to be that way, however. Using overgrazed pastures as an illustration of the results of cattle grazing is like using an extremely obese person as an illustration of the results of eating.

Cattle grazing provides a prairie manager with unique flexibility in determining the timing, frequency, and intensity of the defoliation of plants, and, to some extent, which plants are grazed and which are not. Because cattle are selective feeders (they don't eat everything with equal zeal) they provide op-

While it's no longer camouflaged against the dried grass that was burned, this grasshopper nymph survived the prescribed fire that swept its prairie. Many insects have strategies for surviving fires, but others do not, and it is important to keep them in mind during fire planning.

tions not available with less-selective methods like fire and mowing. They also give you the option of defoliating plants repeatedly throughout the season, which can be important if you are trying to reduce the dominance of those plants in the community.

It's also important to remember that periodic defoliation, whether through grazing or other means, is not fatal for plants. Cattle don't pull plants up by the roots; they just nip off the tops. Perennial plants are built to withstand that kind of stress, even though it may cause them to lose root capacity temporarily or to skip a year of reproduction. Besides, as discussed earlier, weakening perennial plants is one of the key elements of prairie management because it opens up space for the establishment of new plants in the community. Even annual plants can withstand considerable defoliation, and because of their life strategy they are the best suited to rebound (from seed) when the community around them is weakened by grazing.

Cattle grazing can require a significant investment in infrastructure (fences, water facilities, etc.) and time as compared to other management options, but the return on that investment can really be worth it. The amount of infrastructure (fence and water) you need to invest in depends on how you plan to use cattle and whether you own the cattle or are renting your land to a cattle owner. The appendix provides more specific information on fence and livestock watering systems and other aspects of grazing management, such as calculation of appropriate stocking rates. However, if you don't own the cattle, the cattle owner you rent your land to will often be the best source of information for what he/she needs to support his/her cattle.

There are two basic ways to use cattle as a management tool for grasslands. The first is to utilize them infrequently and for short periods of time to address a particular issue (to reduce grass dominance or increase vegetation-structure heterogeneity). In this case, you may not need much for permanent infrastructure, because it's likely you can find a cattle owner who is willing to put up electric fence and haul water to the animals during the short periods they are in your prairie. On the other hand, you may choose to use cattle as a consistent part of your management, in which case some kind of permanent perimeter fence and water source will be necessary. Often there is money available from various government and nongovernment sources to help you set up grazing infrastructure, especially if the grazing will help to improve the quality of a prairie (see the appendix for information on where to go for that kind of assistance). The rest of this chapter will discuss some effective ways to use grazing as an occasional or regular part of your management system.

Periodic cattle grazing can be very effective at addressing some threats to prairie diversity. As an example, putting a lot of cattle in a prairie for the months of April and May can be a great way to reduce the dominance of cool-season exotic grasses like smooth brome, Kentucky bluegrass, or others. The same kind of short-term, high-intensity grazing could also be used in the summer (June–August) if warm-season grasses appear to be overabundant and are reducing plant diversity or habitat structure. Neither of these actions will fix the problem after only one grazing period, but they can provide fairly dramatic results in the short term, and repeated treatments can begin to change the balance of power in the plant community over time.

Regardless of the season, short-term, high-intensity grazing can have a big impact on vegetation structure. Fencing the cattle into a particular section of a prairie, and excluding them from other sections, can result in a dramatic contrast between short and tall vegetation within the same site. Within the grazed section, the combination of short-cropped grass and the disturbance to the soil surface from the hooves of the animals can really increase seed germination. Sometimes, short-term intensive grazing can also be helpful in weed control efforts. Grazing down the tall grass can make the weeds and young trees easier to find, increase the effectiveness of herbicide treatments, and sometimes also weaken the weeds before they are sprayed.

If your goal is to improve vegetation structure for wildlife habitat, it can sometimes be useful to use a less intensive grazing treatment (fewer animals spread out over a larger area). Low-intensity grazing gives cattle the ability to be more selective about which plants they eat, as well as how much of each plant. The result is a very patchy structure in which one plant might be grazed nearly to the ground, its neighbor might be completely untouched, and the plant next to that might have just the top nipped off. On a larger scale, some parts of the prairie will be favored over others, creating larger patches of taller and shorter vegetation. For example, cattle often tend to prefer grazing the tops and bottoms of hills (rather than the side slopes) and in areas near shade and water. The longer the cattle are in the prairie, the more dramatic the structural variations will become.

If you decide that grazing can be a consistent part of your management, there are almost unlimited variations to potential grazing systems. The prairie manager's ability to alter the timing, frequency, location, and intensity of the treatment from year to year or day to day is why grazing is so useful. However, there are some standard grazing systems used in cattle management. Some of them are presented below, along with discussion about the benefits and disadvantages of each and suggestions on how to optimize their impact on biodiversity. With each system, the stocking rate will be a critical variable. Lighter stocking rates allow cattle to be more-selective grazers and result in a patchier vegetation structure. Heavier stocking rates force cattle to eat more than just their favorite plants and will reduce vegetation heterogeneity. The correct stocking rate will depend upon your objectives, and will likely change from year to year. However, consistent overgrazing can degrade a prairie regardless of the grazing system. Particularly when dealing with cattle owned by another person, who may have livestock production as the primary objective, it is important to ensure that your stocking rate is based on a sustainable use of the prairie over a long period of time, and that you are adjusting that rate based on your evaluation of whether or not your objectives are being met.

Season-Long Single-Pasture Grazing

The simplest way to graze cattle in a prairie is to fence the perimeter, provide a source of water, and turn the cattle out to graze. Many range scientists and progressive ranchers dismiss this method as outdated or inferior to rotational grazing systems (discussed below). However, it can still be used effectively and, in fact, can have advantages over other systems.

With season-long single-pasture grazing, cattle will develop movement and grazing patterns over time and, for the most part, will maintain those patterns over the length of a grazing season—or even multiple seasons. Favorite foraging sites will be cropped short repeatedly through the season while other sites will be grazed much less. Uneven forage utilization, because of the tendency of cattle to concentrate grazing near water sources, around shade trees, and where they can best catch summer breezes, is one of the reasons many cattle producers dislike this system. However, from a wildlife habitat standpoint, uneven use equals heterogeneity, which is valuable. Taller grass in the corners of the pasture, far from water or trees, can be nesting habitat for the same bird species that may use the shorter-cropped areas near a windmill for feeding, brood-rearing, or courtship displays.

The disadvantage of uneven use is that, if allowed to continue over several seasons, it can reduce plant diversity. Those areas grazed consistently will become populated only by those species that can withstand that kind of grazing or that cattle refuse to eat. Less-grazed areas can become dominated by grasses and other plants that do best in the absence of disturbance. While diversity can remain high on the pasture scale, it diminishes on the grazing-patch scale. Shifting the locations of more-intense grazing around the pasture, so that every site gets periodic rest, can help retain a higher number of plant species in any one place. Obviously, cross-fencing can force cattle to graze only certain parts of the pasture, discussed below with rotational grazing systems, but there are other ways to encourage cattle to shift their grazing around.

There is some evidence that "grazing lawns," areas that cattle keep short through the season, eventually lose their attractiveness to cattle because the favored plants disappear over multiple seasons. If true, this would create a shifting mosaic of grazing lawns across the prairie over time. Abandoned grazing lawns would likely be dominated by annual, biennial, and less-palatable plants for a while, and then, over several years, would slowly be recolonized by big bluestem and other plants favored by cattle. At some point the plant composition would be such that it would attract cattle grazing again and restart the process. The data on whether or not (and how) this happens is still somewhat sketchy because it is such a slow process. And, even if it does happen, there will still be places where cattle concentrate for grazing regardless of plant composition, because of other benefits like shade, breezes to keep insects away, and proximity to water.

Whether or not cattle shift their favorite grazing spots on their own, it can be advantageous for a manager to help the process along. One easy way to shake things up is to vary the stocking rate from year to year. In years with a high stocking rate, the size and number of grazing lawns will expand to meet the needs of a large herd. If you then reduce the herd size for the next grazing season, the cattle will be unable to maintain all of the lawns because the grass will grow faster than they can eat it. Rather than grazing all of the lawns more lightly than in the previous year, they will tend to choose some areas to keep short and will let others go. This should result in some shifting of heavy use from place to place, although, as just mentioned, they will still maintain some favorites because of other factors like the availability of shade and water.

Another way to persuade cattle to choose new favorite grazing spots is by moving their water, shade, or mineral feeders. If you have multiple water sources, including tanks, ponds, streams, or a combination of these, it may be possible to turn off (or fence out) some of them and leave others available. Shade can be more difficult to move, but it may be possible to fence out corner woodlots temporarily, so that cows will choose other shady places for a while. Also, if multiple shady locations are available, changing the location of water will often influence which shade trees are used. Most cattle owners like to use mineral feeders in the pasture to supplement the micronutrients that help with weight gain, milk production, breeding rates, etc. Mineral feeders are usually small and mobile, and can easily be moved from place to place during or between seasons to encourage variations in grazing patterns.

There may be situations in which cattle consistently seek out and graze a few plant species year after year, regardless of where the plants are within a pasture. Ranchers call these ice cream plants, because cattle really love to eat them and can sometimes eliminate them from a prairie after years of re-peated grazing. When using a season-long, single-pasture grazing system, it is important to make sure that isn't happening. If you see plant species that are never allowed to bloom and/or reproduce, it may be necessary either to fence cattle out of some areas each year to allow those plants to survive in the prai-rie or to shift to another grazing system. However, be sure that cattle are the culprits before you make drastic changes. Often, deer and/or other animals develop the same preference for particular plants, and it can be difficult to tell what's actually eating them. If deer are the problem, simply erecting an elec-tric fence will not solve it.

To summarize, season-long single-pasture grazing can create a mosaic of vegetation structure, particularly with light to moderate stocking rates,

Some biologists believe that marbleseed (false gromwell) has become rare in eastern prairies because of a lack of grazing. Cattle rarely eat it, allowing it to thrive in grazed prairies.

because cattle maintain short vegetation in favorite spots. Patchiness will decrease as the stocking rate increases. Plant diversity can be high across the pasture, but may be low on the scale of a grazing lawn if small-scale grazing patterns are not altered over time. Shifting the grazing intensity by altering the stocking rate and the location of water, shade, or mineral feeders can help to maintain higher plant diversity and vigor. Season-long single-pasture grazing often works best on large pastures (160 acres or more) where any overused areas will be a small percentage of the total area, and where there is room for plant species to persist because of uneven use across space. In smaller pastures, stocking rates have to be very low to prevent homogeneous use of the entire pasture, and even then it can be difficult for highly palatable plant species to escape the perennial grazing that may eventually eliminate them from the site.

Rotational Grazing

Rotational grazing systems are those that move cattle from one part of a pasture to another (or from one pasture to another) over time by using fences to split grazing units (paddocks) from each other. The key element of rotational grazing is that it gives grazed plants a period of undisturbed regrowth following grazing. This can help both to avoid the loss of ice cream plants from repeated continous grazing in a season-long system and to even out the utilization of forage across a pasture. Rather than allowing cattle to develop patterns where portions of a pasture are repeatedly grazed more intensively than others, rotational grazing restricts cattle to a small area until the cattle manager decides to move them. This lets the manager adjust the level of grazing intensity in any one area, and also the length of time between grazing events.

Rotational grazing systems are widely promoted as the best system for both livestock production and "rangeland health." However, that position is not necessarily supported by science. A recent study synthesized a half-century's worth of research testing rotational grazing and concluded that there is no basis for claims that it is better than continuous season-long grazing. In fact, many studies concluded that the opposite was true. Nevertheless, rotational grazing has very strong advocates among university faculty and farmers/ranchers, who insist that it can support higher stocking rates, reduce weed infestations, and lead to better overall soil and prairie conditions. All of those things can occur under rotational grazing, but it is likely that many happen because the livestock operator is paying close attention to the way cattle are grazing, and makes constant adjustments based on those observations—not because the pasture is split into a particular number of paddocks. Rotational grazing is inherently neither a good nor a bad system. It has advantages and disadvantages like any other. If it can help you meet the objectives you have for your prairie, you should consider it. But you should not let anyone convince you that splitting your prairie into smaller pieces is the only way to graze it effectively.

The major advantages of rotational grazing systems come from the ability of the manager to have more control over the location and intensity of grazing. The smaller the paddock (or the higher the stocking rate within the paddock), the more intensive and the less selective the grazing will be. Cattle can be kept in a paddock until the desired grazing impact has been reached, and then be allowed to move to the next. The vegetation in a paddock can then be rested until it has recovered to the desired extent before being grazed again. To some extent, multiple paddocks mean that rest and grazing periods can be flexible, based on weather and other conditions. However, there are only

Many rotational grazing systems with numerous small paddocks are targeted at homogenizing both the grazing pressure across a site and the plant community itself.

a limited number of paddocks available in a particular rotational system, so moving out of one paddock sooner than planned because of drought, for example, means that another paddock will get less rest than planned.

There are also some disadvantages to rotational grazing, particularly from habitat- and species-diversity perspectives. Because rotational grazing favors uniform use of forage within paddocks, the heterogeneity of vegetation structure is reduced. In cases where vegetation is kept short and paddocks are grazed on a frequent basis, the system often favors cool-season invasive grasses over native warm-season grasses. In more extreme rotations, where many animals are moved quickly through many small paddocks, wildlife can sometimes suffer, both from trampling (nests, young, etc.) and from the fragmentation of the prairie by numerous fences. Finally, the goal of rotational grazing from the standpoint of cattle production is often a fairly homogeneous plant community, dominated by those species most palatable and nutritious to cattle—primarily grasses. Obviously, a homogeneous plant community is not desirable if biodiversity and wildlife habitat are major objectives.

However, there are numerous ways to set up a rotational system. The number of paddocks can vary from as few as two to as many as someone is willing to construct. The intensity of grazing each paddock gets, the frequency with which it gets grazed, and the length of rest can all be varied, depending upon objectives. Rest-rotation, or deferred-rotation, systems allow some paddocks to skip a cycle or two periodically and rest for an entire season or longer.

From a biodiversity standpoint, more flexibility and less repetition are important facets of a successful rotational grazing system. A three-paddock system, where each paddock is grazed for a third of the season, is a common setup. Even if the first paddock to be used changes each year, the plant community is still subjected to a repetitive pattern of early grazing one year, midseason grazing the next, and late season grazing the next. Periodically changing the order of grazing to shake up that pattern can help keep the plant community from adapting to a set pattern of disturbances. This might include the occasional grazing of one paddock twice in the same year (spring and fall) while resting another completely. In addition, changing the length of time each paddock is grazed from year to year can also help. Adding paddocks so that the rotation runs on a 5- or 6-year cycle rather than 3 years may decrease the likelihood that a plant community will conform to a simple repetitive cycle. However, smaller paddocks can also mean more-even utilization, decreasing habitat-structure heterogeneity and, potentially, plant diversity.

An ideal rotational grazing system for biodiversity management allows the manager to make decisions about when and where cattle will graze based on his/her objectives for vegetation structure and to change those plans as conditions change. For example, some paddocks might need to be grazed early in the season for several years in a row to combat a cool-season exotic grass problem. Other paddocks may benefit from full-season rest or, conversely, may need summer grazing to release forb species from dominance by warm-season grasses. In some years a high stocking rate may be needed throughout, and in other years a low stocking rate.

Rotational grazing was developed primarily for cattle production. To that end, it is normally used as a way to homogenize use of vegetation across the pasture and to favor highly palatable species. Both of those are counter to bio-diversity objectives. However, having multiple options for where to put cattle (or where to exclude them) at different times can be useful for biodiversity management. The best possible scenario is to have a wide range of options, including paddocks that are flexible in size; rotations that are flexible in terms of timing, frequency, and intensity; and the ability to change a rotation in midstream to adapt to changing conditions. These ideas will be explored more in the next section.

Controlled Random Grazing

Controlled random grazing is a way to use the advantages of various graz-ing systems without being locked into any particular one. In some ways, controlled random grazing is not really a grazing system at all. It's more of a management philosophy that allows a manager maximum flexibility to shift disturbances around in a prairie to prevent repetition, counteract perceived threats from invasive species, and meet short-term and long-term objectives.

In controlled random grazing, the grazing plans for a particular year are based on a combination of two factors. First, the manager looks back at the previous several years of management to see what kinds of timing, intensity, and duration of grazing have been used in various parts of the prairie. Then he/she evaluates the condition of the prairie (the vigor of dominant plant species; the abundance, density, and location of various invasive species; the abundance of disturbance-dependent plant species; and the vegetation struc-ture). Then, combining the recent management history and the current condi-tion, the manager sets a grazing plan for the upcoming season.

Electric fence can be an essential component of a good controlled random grazing system. The prairie can be sectioned off in a different way each year (or not at all in some years) to meet specific objectives. Areas with smooth brome dominance can be fenced off so that they can be grazed hard in the spring and rested in the summer. Portions that need complete rest for a pe-riod can be fenced out. Grazing units can shift location from year to year and overlap with each other over time to eliminate any permanent boundaries. The number of potential grazing-unit configurations is limited only by the need to include a water facility in each unit that gets grazed.

Temporary electric fences can contain cattle effectively in some areas while resting others, and they are relatively inexpensive and easy to construct.

In one year, the entire prairie could be grazed as a single pasture with a light stocking rate as a way to encourage the development of patchy vegetation structure. The next year, one-third of the prairie with a particularly heavy stand of smooth brome might be sectioned off so that it is grazed early in the season and rested for the remainder. In that same year, another third could be grazed hard for the summer and fall, while the remaining third is rested completely. The following year might see the prairie rested entirely or not, depending upon its condition and the objectives of the manager.

Although controlled random grazing has many advantages, it has disadvantages as well. Changing the electric fence configuration each year takes a lot of work, not only to set up fence, but also to fix it repeatedly after deer and other animals run into, over, or through it each time you change its location. It can be harder to evaluate particular strategies over time when they are never used in the same way (or location) twice. And it can be difficult to change the number of cattle used in the prairie from year to year, regardless of whether you own the cattle or rent the pasture to someone else.

Grazing a prairie is useful only if it meets objectives. If your objectives are to maximize biodiversity and wildlife habitat, flexibility is critical. Dry years and wet years will each require alterations in stocking rate and grazing patterns to keep the prairie condition as you want it. Because it's not yet possible to predict whether a year will be wet or dry before it starts, stocking rate (and other management decisions) can really only be based on the weather from the previous year—in addition to the vigor and condition of the prairie. The controlled random approach allows you not only to alter management from year to year, but also to change your mind midseason if you don't like the response you're getting from the vegetation.

Management with Both Fire and Grazing

Some ecologists now argue that fire and grazing should be seen as part of the same natural disturbance because, historically, fire would have almost always been followed by intensive grazing of some kind. In prairie management, there are impacts from the combination of fire and grazing that are not seen when the techniques are used independently. Among other things, grazing following fire can help to counter any increased grass productivity and to aid in the germination and establishment of new plants from seeds.

Controlled Random Fire and Grazing

One way to take advantage of the benefits of combining fire and grazing is to simply add fire to the controlled random approach discussed earlier. In addition to varying the grazing timing, location, intensity, frequency, etc., you can use fire as well. For example, in one year you might burn half of the prairie in the early spring, follow that with intensive grazing on the same area to suppress smooth brome regrowth, and then shift the cattle to the other half for the summer period. The next year you might burn a third of the prairie in the late spring to suppress Kentucky bluegrass, and exclude it from grazing to encourage warm-season plants to reassert dominance. The potential configurations and options only increase when both fire and grazing are available. Fire can be added as a component to season-long single-pasture or rotational

Cattle are grazing here on recently burned prairie in a patch-burn grazing system. The forage quality of the fresh regrowth of grasses is so high that cattle begin grazing the grass as soon as it emerges.

grazing systems too, as long as the grazing system allows enough vegetation growth to enable a fire to burn through it. This can add benefits such as eastern redcedar control and removal of litter to aid in seed germination.

Patch-burn Grazing

Patch-burn grazing, a relatively new idea for combining fire and grazing, is showing great promise for its biodiversity benefits. It captures much of the dynamism of the controlled random management philosophy, but wraps it into a more comprehensive, but still flexible, system. The method was originally conceived as a way to manage large bison herds on lands owned by The Nature Conservancy. It is now being tested and used with cattle on much smaller pastures. So far, the method appears to create great heterogeneous vegetation structure for wildlife habitat and increase plant diversity without compromising livestock performance.

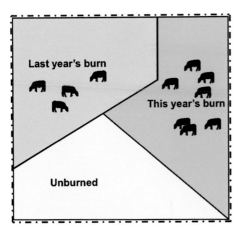
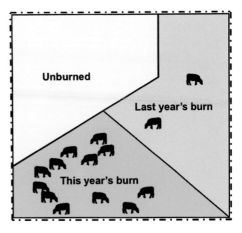

Figure 9. Patch-burn grazing. The only fence is around the outside of the large pasture. The cattle spend most of their time in the current year's burn patch and spill over into last year's burn periodically. A different patch is burned the next year and the cattle change their grazing pattern to follow the fire.

Patch-burn grazing encourages intensive grazing on a portion of a pasture each year while resting, or lightly grazing, the remainder of the pasture. Each year, a portion of the pasture is burned (the burn patch), which attracts grazing cattle to the lush regrowth of grass following the fire (figure 9). Cattle concentrate their grazing within the burn patch until a new patch is burned—usually the following year. The location of the next burn is often determined by where there is sufficient fuel available to carry a fire. That fuel includes dead grass, either standing or lying on the ground. Once the latest burn starts to green up, cattle mostly ignore the previous burn patch and concentrate their grazing in the new area. That allows the grasses and forbs in the previous burn patch to begin recovering until they are tall and dense enough to carry another fire.

While patch-burn grazing has some similarities to traditional rotational grazing, the biggest difference is that patch-burn grazing doesn't require any

interior fencing. Cattle concentrate their grazing in the most recently burned patch because of the highly nutritious grass that regrows after the fire, but they are not fenced into that patch. When grass growth slows down in times of hot dry weather or cool wet weather, cattle are able to move into the previous year's burn and graze lightly until the current year's burn catches up again. The extent to which the cattle spill over into the previous year's burn is determined by stocking rate. They will spill over more under higher stocking rates, and less under lower stocking rates.

It may be the ability of cattle to forage outside of the burn patch when grass regrowth falls behind grazing pressure that creates one of the most intriguing results of patch-burn grazing. For a long time, it has been accepted as fact that cattle and bison choose their diets very differently in prairies. Research has shown that forbs typically make up less than 10 percent of the diet of bison, as opposed to 10–20 percent for cattle. Several prairie forbs have been considered at risk because cattle seem to favor them. However, in the patch-burn grazing system, cattle eat almost the same diet as bison. Under light stocking rates (50–75 percent of what an agricultural producer might typically use), forb species that have always been seen as favorites of cattle are rarely grazed, even within the burn patch. Under moderate stocking rates (what a conservative agricultural producer would use), cattle may graze many of those forb species in the burned patch, but they tend not to graze them in the previous year's patch or the unburned area. This shift in grazing preferences has tremendous potential to increase forb diversity in prairies over time. Several research projects are currently under way to see whether that actually happens.

The other big difference between patch-burn grazing and most other rotational grazing systems is in the grazing intensity between portions of the pasture. In most rotational systems, the goal is usually to graze a paddock (a fenced-in unit of the pasture) until only the lower leaves of the grasses remain and then move to the next one. The first paddock is then allowed to rest, and the leaves left on the grass plants allow them to recover relatively quickly from the grazing period. In addition, it's common to try to regraze that paddock before the grasses get too tall and rank because the forage quality goes

Patch-burn grazing at light stocking rates can induce cattle to be very selective grazers, focusing mainly on grasses. This can help forbs and other plants gain an advantage over dominant grasses, thereby increasing plant diversity.

down. The result is a series of paddocks in which the grass heights are never too short or too tall, and uniform throughout each paddock.

In contrast, the burn patch in a patch-burn grazing system is grazed for an entire season at a very high intensity, and most grasses are kept almost at ground level for most of that time. Meanwhile, the unburned portions of the pasture are in various stages of recovery from previous years of intensive grazing. Recently burned patches are dominated by annual weeds and annual and perennial forbs, and have thin, weakened stands of grass. Patches that have rested for longer periods have tall, dense vegetation structure where grass has reasserted dominance. So, in contrast to rotational grazing, patch-burn grazing subjects a prairie to extended periods of intensive grazing followed by multiyear rest periods, creating a very heterogeneous array of vegetation structure across the pasture.

That vegetation structure provides excellent habitat for a wide variety of wildlife species. The short vegetation in the burn patch is perfect for birds like upland sandpipers that prefer open areas for either nesting or feeding. In unburned areas where little grazing has occurred for 2 or more years, the grasses and other plants grow tall and thick. This provides dense vegetation for rare species like Henslow's sparrows, and excellent nesting and wintering habitat for game birds like bobwhite quail. It also provides adequate fuel for the next fire, and ensures that the fire will burn with sufficient intensity to kill trees such as eastern redcedars.

In the patch burned during the previous year, grasses slowly recover their vigor. In the meantime, both annual and perennial plants move into open spaces left by the weakened grasses, increasing their abundance by both seed and rhizomes. This weedy-looking vegetation structure provides ideal (and unique) brood-rearing habitat for upland game birds like pheasants and quail. Young birds have the safety provided by vertical cover (tall forbs), and the lack of dense grass near the ground allows them to move freely under that cover to feed and escape danger. Many other wildlife species also benefit from the habitat and food quantities provided by the vegetation response to the fire and grazing, including species of reptiles, amphibians, and insects, all of which can easily meet their thermoregulation needs in areas of abundant food.

Under a patch-burn system, there is almost no grazing in the unburned patch of a prairie, allowing plants to recover their vigor and build fuel for the next burn.

While the impact on the plant community is still being tested, it does appear that plant diversity increases through the patch-burn grazing system, particularly under a relatively light stocking rate. Under that scenario, most grasses within the burned patch are cropped very short and kept that way for the entire season, but most forbs are left ungrazed. The ability of those forbs to grow vigorously while grasses are being suppressed by grazing provides them with a competitive edge. Seed germination and seedling survival rates of plants other than the dominant grasses are high during both the year of the burn and the next year, because the weakened grasses allow more light to hit the ground and take up less root space below ground.

Under a higher stocking rate, including a rate that would be economically sustainable for a farmer or rancher, there is very little selectivity by the grazing cattle within the burned patch. In other words, the cattle eat almost everything. This might seem, at first, to be counterproductive if plant diversity is the goal, but that's not necessarily the case. In some cases, uniform grazing within the burned patch means that species that are becoming too dominant (including invasive species) because they are normally avoided by cattle may become less dominant. Species such as sericea lespedeza, an invasive forb found mainly in the southern half of the tallgrass prairie, gain an edge in pastures because their high levels of tannins make them less attractive to grazing cattle. Under the intensive grazing that occurs in a burned patch, those species get grazed early in the season, before tannin levels get too high, and then are grazed repeatedly for much of the season as they try to regrow. This resets the playing field in a way that takes the competitive edge away from those species. In Oklahoma, researchers are finding that pastures under patch-burn grazing experience a much lower rate of increase of sericea lespedeza than pastures under other grazing systems. Patch-burning doesn't seem to solve the problem, but it may be a big part of a solution.

Of course, the nonselective grazing seen under higher stocking rates means that rare plant species and others that you might want to see increase in abundance may get grazed within the burned patch too. This may or may not be a problem. It's likely that those species will not be grazed in the unburned portions of the prairie, so they will have several years to recover. Most prairie plants can withstand periodic grazing without any problems. However, the

The selective grazing and heterogeneity of vegetation structure in patch-burn grazing benefit both plant diversity and wildlife habitat.

use of patch-burn grazing (or any kind of grazing) on high-quality prairies for conservation purposes is still a fairly recent phenomenon, and you will have to judge for yourself whether or not it furthers your objectives.

In prairies that are already being grazed, or which have a history of grazing, there may be forb species, highly preferred by cattle, that have become rare because of years of chronic defoliation. In those situations, patch-burn grazing could help those species recover because they would now be grazed only in the burned patch, and have two or more years to recover and reproduce until the same area is burned again. If the historical stocking rate was reasonable, the same number of cattle, but under a patch-burn grazing scenario, might lead to a more diverse prairie community.

The key to whether or not plant diversity will increase lies in the recovery period between fire and grazing events. At least three things need to happen. First, plant species normally suppressed by the dominant vegetation must be released from that competition and temporarily expand their territories through either seed or rhizomes. Second, native plants that are especially favored by cattle must be given sufficient time to recover after grazing and be able to reproduce often enough to sustain their populations. Finally, invasive species must not win the race to fill in the space opened by intensive grazing. In many prairies, the biggest threat to diversity comes from cool-season exotic grasses like smooth brome, Kentucky bluegrass, and tall fescue. If those species aren't suppressed sufficiently by the fire/grazing, or recover more quickly than native plants, the system will not favor plant diversity. Some options for modifying patch-burn grazing to better target those cool-season grasses are listed later in this chapter.

One of the most encouraging signs for patch-burn grazing is that it appears to be at least equivalent to other grazing systems in terms of livestock performance. Oklahoma State University has been tracking the differences in the way cattle respond to patch-burn grazing as compared to other common livestock systems. So far, there are no differences in average daily weight gains or any other measures. In addition, a stocking rate that is sustainable in other grazing systems can also be applied to patch-burn grazing, so it is not necessarily important to reduce cattle numbers when switching to patch-burn grazing. These findings should help prairie managers who must convince wary tenants to try a new system, as well as encourage prairie owners who have their own cattle.

While patch-burn grazing seems to have a lot of promise as a management system, it is like any other system in that you can modify and adapt it to fit your particular objectives. Building temporary exclosures with electric fence, removing cattle and/or fire for entire seasons, changing the length of the grazing season, altering the timing of fires, and varying the stocking rate between or within seasons are just a few ways to adjust the system. Like other grazing systems, patch-burn grazing is more a tool than a recipe, so use it in ways that fit your needs.

Much of the benefit of patch-burn grazing to plant communities comes from the level of selectivity shown by the grazing cattle. Under a light stocking rate, cattle show high selectivity, choosing to graze primarily in the most recently burned patch, and also choosing grasses over forbs. While we don't completely understand the reason for the increase in grazing selectivity, it probably relates to the fact that while cattle do concentrate most of their grazing in a small part of the prairie, they have the option to leave that area when they want or need to. That allows them to optimize their diet as they want and to ignore these plants that they would ordinarily not choose.

However, under a higher stocking rate, cattle are still selective in that they graze primarily in the burned patch, but they are not very selective about what they eat within that patch. In that case, the high number of cattle means that they can't satisfy themselves by eating only their favorite plants. Rather than searching the entire prairie for those favored plants, cattle prefer to graze all or most of the plant species within the burned patch. Both high and low stocking rates can create situations that benefit prairie plant communities. The important point is to use the grazing selectivity created by patch-burn grazing in a way that furthers your objectives. Following are a few specific ideas on how you could modify the patch-burn system to fit your particular needs.

It isn't clear yet what the potential is for patch-burn grazing to help with the control of invasive grasses like smooth brome or tall fescue. There are at least two strategies currently being tested that attempt to maintain the core patch-burn grazing idea while targeting dominant cool-season exotic grasses. The first combines early spring grazing with a late spring fire. Under that scenario, grazing begins early in the season but the new burn patch is created in the late spring, while the cattle are already in the pasture. If cattle are in the pasture when cool-season grasses are just starting to grow, they should graze those grasses (mainly in the previous year's burn patch) until the current year's patch is burned (late April to mid May). Once the new burn patch greens up, the cattle should shift out of the previous year's burn patch into the current year's burn for the remainder of the season. If a third of the pasture is burned each year, cool-season grasses will be negatively affected on two-thirds of the site each spring (by the spring grazing on the previous year's burn patch and the fire on this year's patch). Meanwhile, native warm-season

grasses will only be negatively affected in one-third of the site (summer grazing in this year's burn patch). Over time, that may shift the balance of power from cool-season exotic grasses toward native plants.

In this late spring burn scenario it may be important to have cattle out of the pasture by early to mid September to avoid too much grazing in the next year's burn patch, particularly with higher stocking rates. Especially during a dry fall, the grass in the current year's burn patch will slow or even stop its growth at the end of the warm-season grass season (August). Following that, cattle spread out and graze much more widely across the remaining part of the pasture, creating patches of grazed vegetation here and there. If they are allowed to continue this for a long enough time at a sufficiently high stocking rate, they could reduce the fuel load enough that next year's late spring fire will not burn well.

A second strategy being tested to help suppress cool-season grasses involves reducing the stocking rate as the season progresses. The idea is to put more grazing pressure on grasses during the spring than the summer, with the hope of tipping the balance of dominance away from cool-season grasses. In this scenario, a dormant-season fire can be used to create the next burn patch. When the cattle come into the pasture in April, they should be at a high enough stocking rate that they will graze intensively both the very recent burn and the previous year's burn patch. Then, about late May, or before the warm-season grasses get very far along in their growth cycle, the stocking rate in the pasture should be cut back by one-third to one-half. The hope is that the remaining cattle will then spend most of their time in the current year's burn patch while abandoning last year's burn patch and allowing it and the unburned patch to rest for the summer. As with the first scenario, the idea is to suppress cool-season grasses on two-thirds of the site but to suppress warm-season grasses on only one-third each year.

If cool-season grasses are really dominant, it may be important either to address that dominance first before beginning a long-term patch-burn

One method being tested for controlling invasive cool-season grasses is to put cows in the prairie in the early spring and then burn in the late spring. Cattle are present during the burn, which requires extra caution during fires but does not generally present big problems.

grazing regime or to modify the patch-burn system even more. One option would be to conduct a late spring fire on a larger-than-normal patch each year and then fence cattle out of part of that burned area to allow warm-season grasses to thrive. The location of the enclosure could be changed each year to allow different areas to rest during the summer. Or, it might be necessary periodically to suspend the patch-burn grazing system for a year and employ a late spring fire or intensive early grazing (or both) followed by summer rest for the entire site.

Regardless of the method you try to reduce the dominance of cool-season exotic grasses, treat it as a restoration technique rather than a long-term management strategy. Suppressing cool-season exotic grasses with fire and/or grazing will also suppress many native plants that grow at the same time of year. Losing those native plant species is counterproductive if you're trying to increase plant diversity. And changing from a prairie dominated by cool-season exotic grasses to one dominated by warm-season native grasses isn't necessarily better either. You're just exchanging one simplified plant community for another. It's unlikely that you'll be able to eradicate cool-season exotic grasses from your prairie, so go ahead and target them when they appear to be overly dominant, but don't do the same thing every year. In years when the exotic grasses are less dominant, change your management to allow native cool-season plants to recover.

There are other ways to make use of the benefits of patch-burn grazing. In most places where this system is used, about a third of the pasture is burned each year. However, in drier climates, for example, it might be valuable or necessary to reduce that fire frequency. The potential disadvantage of doing so may be that you get less-frequent grazing and/or fire suppression of cool-season exotic grasses or other invasive species, but it would provide vegetation a longer rest period before being burned and grazed again.

In addition to fire frequency, the season of fire can be modified as well. For example, summer fires usually favor forbs over grasses, so it may be useful to incorporate them periodically. On the other hand, summer fires can also favor cool-season exotic grasses—at least in situations where fire is used without grazing—and summer fire in patch-burn grazed systems hasn't been well tested yet in prairies where cool-season exotics are a big threat. Experimenting with fall fires as opposed to spring fires may also prove valuable. Patches burned in the fall and left barren during the winter will capture less moisture and expose shallow plant roots to frost more than will vegetated areas, something that could produce either positive or negative results. In addition, bare patches may favor some wildlife species, by creating winter foraging areas for birds like longspurs and early spring courtship-display sites for prairie-chickens, but will obviously not provide winter cover for bobwhite quail.

Experimenting with the type of livestock being used could provide valuable information as well. Even just trading cow-calf pairs for yearlings may change the way the grazing affects the plant community. Mature cows are more experienced foragers and choose a greater variety of plants than inexperienced yearlings. Those diet choices may have advantages or disadvantages, depending upon the site. Yearling cattle may also provide more flexibility in terms of the grazing season than cow-calf pairs. Yearlings can be bought, sold, or moved to the feedlot at any time of year, depending on the needs of the cattle owner, which allows flexibility on the timing of cattle coming in and out of the pasture, whereas cow-calf pairs need pasture for the entire season.

In summary, patch-burn grazing can be seen as a slightly more regulated version of a controlled random fire/grazing system. The shifting pattern of fire, followed by grazing, is probably similar to the kind of regime under which prairie plants evolved. But more important, it seems to provide the kind of disturbance regime that today's prairies need to maintain vigor and diversity. There is probably no upper limit to the size of pasture that can be used, and the lower limit is most likely defined by the size of pasture needed to support the smallest stocking rate possible (one cow). The periodic fire in patch-burn grazing provides help with controlling invasive trees, may help suppress cool-season exotic grasses and other weeds, and stimulates vegetation growth and seedling establishment. At the same time, grazing prevents grasses from becoming too dominant following a fire, creates heterogeneous vegetation structure, and further helps to foster a diverse plant community. There is no set protocol to follow with patch-burn grazing. Like the other management options listed in this section, it is an idea that should be considered within an adaptive management regime designed to meet your individual objectives.

Grazing with Other Livestock (Sheep, Goats, Horses, etc.)

Cattle are obviously not the only domestic livestock that can be used in prairie management. Sheep, goats, horses, llamas, bison, and others may be available, depending upon your particular situation. Still, apart from bison, very little information is available on how to use other livestock to manage prairies for biodiversity. Goats are often noted for their potential to help with invasive species, and they will be discussed in that context later. Because sheep tend to favor forbs over grasses, or at least to graze more forbs than cattle do, they are also sometimes used to help control invasive broad-leaved plants. However, they may not be the best fit for a long-term management strategy if plant diversity is a goal, because they can reduce forb diversity. Horses are difficult to evaluate because they are rarely used as the only livestock in a pasture, except in very small paddocks where they are supplemented with hay because there is insufficient grass. In the rare cases where horses are kept in large pastures, no one seems to have evaluated their potential for managing plant diversity. The biggest knock against horses is that the way their mouth structure works tends to rip, rather than clip, vegetation. This can mean that they pull plants out by the roots rather more often than do other livestock. But in spite of these issues, there is no reason not to experiment with other livestock if it's available, and many of the principles that apply to good biodiversity-friendly grazing management should still apply.

Cattle or Bison?

One question—why not use bison instead of cattle?—often arises in discussions about the use of grazing for biodiversity-friendly prairie management. It's true that bison are the species that prairies evolved with over thousands of years. And there are some differences between the way bison and cattle graze and behave. However, bison come with their own set of challenges as well, and may or may not be a good fit for individual situations.

First, as we learn more about patch-burn grazing and other systems that allow cattle to graze more like historical bison did (free selection of forage over a large mosaic of burned and unburned areas), we are finding that their forage selection is more similar to that of bison than previously thought. Similarly, when bison are put into grazing systems typically used by cattle (e.g., rota-

Bison, like these on The Nature Conservancy's Broken Kettle Grasslands in Iowa, fit well into large grasslands but can present logistical difficulties in small prairies.

tional grazing on relatively small pastures), they graze more as we typically think of cattle grazing, in terms of their forage selection.

However, there are some important differences between bison and cattle, mainly in habitat use. One is their use of shade and water. During the hot part of the summer, cattle like to cool off by sitting in water and under trees. This can cause ecological concerns when they stomp around (and defecate in) the same wetland, pond, or stream each year. They can also stomp and graze areas near trees into nearly bare dirt, which can be a problem if there are rare plants or communities trying to grow there. Bison don't generally spend time sitting in water or in the shade. If anything, they'll use a tree as a good place to scratch an itchy coat, but then move on. Cattle also have the tendency to walk in single file lines along consistently used trails. This can cause problems over time if the trails are always in the same places, especially where soil erosion is a concern.

While these differences are important, they can be mitigated with careful thought. Sensitive wetlands and streams can be fenced out periodically, or permanently if necessary. The same can be done with shade trees and any sensitive areas around them. In addition, many of the ideas presented earlier to redistribute the grazing pressure of cattle can also help to keep them from overusing the same water or shady areas of a pasture every year. Moving drinking water or mineral feeders, or burning a different portion of the pasture each year, can concentrate animals in different places from season to season and avoid consistent overuse. It can also change the patterns of daily movement, helping to avoid the establishment of perennial trails that might cause erosion problems.

The people most knowledgeable about the use of bison in prairie conservation suggest that there may be a minimum pasture size of about 5,000 acres for bison, below which cattle may be a better option. Historically, bison had the ability to roam over hundreds of miles in search of forage, a situation not likely to be replicated again. Larger pastures, though, provide them with greater opportunities to act like bison than smaller pastures. More important, bison in smaller pastures can present logistical challenges that make them less feasible than cattle. Bison are more likely than cattle to push through a fence to get somewhere they want to go. In larger pastures they are much more apt to be satisfied inside their fence than in smaller pastures, and when they feel the need to stampede (which they do periodically) they are less likely to stampede through a fence. In addition, the other infrastructure required to maintain a bison herd, including corrals for legally required annual vaccinations and for sorting cull animals, is expensive and may not be economically worthwhile for a small pasture and/or herd. Despite all of that, there are people who raise bison successfully in relatively small pastures. If you are considering that, be sure to consider carefully all the ramifications of that decision, and don't assume that you will improve your prairie simply by using bison rather than cattle.

Thus far, chapters in this section have dealt primarily with management strategies aimed at creating and maintaining diverse plant communities. By and large, those strategies will also result in diverse and heterogeneous habitat structure. However, there are ways to pay additional attention to the habitat needs of particular species if they are of interest to you, or in need of special conservation. It's not that you need to devise a new and different management strategy for these species, but more that you can keep their requirements in mind as you adapt your plant-diversity-oriented management from year to year. And it's important to remember that you may not have to provide every kind of habitat these species need, especially in landscapes where there are lots of relatively small landholdings together. If you can look over your fences to see what your neighbors are providing in terms of habitat structure, you can often make simple adjustments to your own habitat to provide missing components.

Remnant-Dependent Insects

There are many ways to categorize insects with regard to their value or need for conservation. For example, Ron Panzer and other biologists in the Chicago area have begun keeping track of insect species that they term "remnant-dependent"—they are found almost exclusively in intact prairies, as opposed

The Gorgone checkerspot butterfly is classified as a rare and remnant-dependent insect in eastern tallgrass prairies but is more common in the west where habitat fragmentation is less severe.

to gardens, fields, tame pastures, or other places. These species are particularly vulnerable to loss of prairie habitat and to the way such habitat is managed, because if they are eliminated from one site, there are very few other sites from which they can recolonize. Leafhoppers and other species that aren't able to travel long distances are especially likely to be at risk, but the group of remnant-dependent insects includes many others, even mobile species like butterflies.

The classification of remnant-dependent insects is most important in the eastern portions of tallgrass prairie where landscape fragmentation is especially severe. Further west, high-quality prairies are more likely to be near other native grasslands, even if those grasslands are relatively degraded. For at least some insects, that kind of landscape is much friendlier and can facilitate movement and colonization better than a few little prairies surrounded by miles and miles of rowcrop agriculture and urban sprawl. In highly fragmented landscapes, keeping the needs of insect species in mind is critical when making management decisions. For example, burning an entire prairie could kill all the individuals of a particular species. And that can happen even with dormant-season fires because many insects overwinter above ground, as adults, larvae, or eggs.

There are many conflicting ideas about how best to manage small, isolated prairies for insect conservation, in part because we know so little about most prairie insects. Some people advocate for not using fire as a tool at all, or for at least leaving portions of the prairie unburned for long periods of time. Unfortunately, as with all management strategies, there are multiple tradeoffs. Reducing fire frequency or eliminating fire from some areas creates other issues, including an increase in woody plant invasion that can reduce plant diversity—which, in turn, affects insect diversity. In general, the best advice for owners of small, isolated prairies is to be thoughtful about management decisions and to avoid blanket applications of fire or haying that don't leave any areas of standing vegetation from which insects can recolonize.

Grassland Birds

As discussed earlier, grassland birds have habitat requirements unique to each species. Some, like horned larks, thrive on nearly bare ground while others, like sedge wrens, prefer tall, dense grass. In prairie landscapes, or where management of private lands is dominated by relatively intense grazing, the missing habitat component is often tall, rank vegetation that hasn't had fire or grazing for several years. By contrast, in some eastern rural landscapes, grasslands may be hayed or burned but are rarely grazed and often are split into smaller pieces by wooded edges. This can create a lack of short-cropped habitat or, more important, short-to-midheight heterogeneous structure.

Species like upland sandpipers tend to do well in western prairie regions where large short-cropped grasslands dominate, but they become rare in small eastern prairies where grasslands are smaller, grazing is less common, vegetation structure is relatively homogeneous, and wooded edges make the

Henslow's sparrows require tall vegetation and abundant litter from previous years' plant growth as nesting habitat. This habitat type is not commonly found in most grasslands because it requires rest periods longer than most agricultural landowners typically use.

landscape feel less open. Henslow's sparrows, by contrast, tend to do just fine in tall, rank, even shrubby, prairies but are not often found in heavily grazed pastures. If a diverse grassland bird community is one of your objectives, do some research to find out which species are rare in your area. You can often find this information by talking to representatives of your state wildlife agency or a local conservation group, or by looking on the Internet for breeding bird survey results or similar data. Learn what the rare species in your area need for habitat, and then see what you can do within your management to provide more of it. In some cases, it might be necessary or helpful to collaborate with neighbors on habitat-structure plans.

Just to make the situation more complex, there are a number of bird species, such as loggerhead shrikes, orchard orioles, Bell's vireos, and brown thrashers, that are often associated with prairies but require shrubby habitat as well. Many of these shrub species have suffered population declines in recent years because both grassland and shrubby habitats have become scarcer. In grasslands of over 50 acres or so, allowing small patches of shrubby habitat while still maintaining large areas with no trees or shrubs could provide for both grass- and shrub-nesting species. However, shrub patches tend to grow larger over time, so constant vigilance will be necessary to ensure that they don't become too large or dominant. Also, shrub patches often allow invasive tree species an easy foothold, because they can germinate and grow in relative security under the shrubs. Be sure to monitor shrub patches carefully for these invading trees.

Managing for grassland birds, then, can be a complicated challenge. It's not possible to have every species present in the same type of habitat, because different species need different kinds of vegetation structure. However, if you can provide a diversity of structure types within a large open prairie, it's likely that a diversity of grassland bird species will come and nest successfully. Paying attention to the kinds of vegetation structure that exists in neighboring grasslands and providing something different on your own land can also help to increase the overall diversity of birds in your neighborhood.

Finally, preventing trees from breaking up your grassland into smaller pieces may be the most important thing you can do for grassland birds. Often the first place trees become a problem is along fencelines or shrub patches where seeds are dropped by perching birds or caught by tall vegetation as they blow across the landscape. Patrolling these areas and removing unneeded fences can make a big difference to the grassland birds using your site.

For those people interested in maintaining large populations of game bird species such as pheasants and quail, the guidance from game biologists has changed fairly dramatically in the last decade or so. Historically, upland game bird management was largely about fall and winter habitat, and emphasized the creation of habitat edges—mosaics of grass cover, food plots, and shrub and tree plantings. The result was that in addition to the creation of numerous small grass/tree/food plot habitats in the corners of center pivot fields and elsewhere, many native grasslands were fragmented and degraded by the addition of tilled food plots, tree plantings, and even interseedings of nonnative legumes and other species.

The current management guidelines for pheasants and quail focus more on breeding habitat, and align better with good overall prairie management. Biologists have found that grass plantings or prairies that go ungrazed or without other management can become too dense even for nesting. Brood-rearing habitat is also very difficult to find in prairies that haven't had some kind of relatively intense disturbance (grazing, disking, burning, etc.). While food plots are still appropriate in rare cases, they serve more to concentrate birds for hunters than anything else, though they may also increase survival during very severe winters. If you do decide to utilize food plots, consider very carefully the location (avoid tilling remnant prairie vegetation or installing shrubs or trees in the middle of open grassland), and do not use plant species with the potential to become invasive.

Today, the most important habitat factor to most professional pheasant and quail managers is the presence of some weedy or "forby" brood cover, with an abundance of annual and/or biennial plants that attract or produce lots of insects. In prairies and planted grasslands, weedy cover can be created by intensive grazing or other disturbances that suppress the dominant grasses and release forbs. It can also be created by fallowing nearby cropfields. Weedy cover provides an abundance of food, can be excellent brood-rearing habitat, and can also provide good winter cover when it includes dense stands of tall, robust weeds like annual sunflowers or giant ragweed.

Patch-burn grazing or other prairie management strategies that mix intensive disturbances with rest periods are very compatible with pheasant and quail management. The entirety of pheasant habitat requirements can be met on prairies with patch-burn grazing. Quail also do very well in a patch-burn system, but may still require dense, shrubby habitat patches dotted around the landscape. In most cases, there are few conflicts between good prairie intensive management and management for pheasants and quail. The biggest potential conflicts are when managers fragment grassland by adding too much woody cover or when they introduce nonnative plant species in an effort to improve habitat. In most landscapes, some of the habitat needs of game birds are present, and a smart land manager can fill in the missing components. Many times, neighboring landowners will provide cropfields and shrubby habitats, and the missing components are dense nesting cover and brood-rearing habitats (in other words, a well-managed native prairie).

There is one final thing to remember about managing for grassland birds. Just because you see lots of birds using your prairie doesn't necessarily mean that they are breeding successfully. You can watch for signs that the birds are raising young. Parents carrying food for a couple of weeks in a row or fledglings learning to fly are good indicators of success. You can help ensure success by making your prairie as functionally large as possible—removing trees, fencelines, and other obstacles that help predators or cowbirds find nests. In addition, make sure that your management strategies aren't counterproductive for nesting success. Grazing systems that concentrate large numbers of animals in small places greatly increase the chance that nests and nestlings will get trampled. Haying a prairie in the early summer can destroy nests and kill nestlings. Even after young birds have fledged, recent research has shown, they tend to stay in the same prairie during the several weeks it takes them to perfect their flying technique. This means that they are still vulnerable to fast-moving hay equipment or to predators after haying removes their protective cover. However, knowing all this should not prevent you from doing the kind of management needed to maintain a diverse prairie. It's important to balance the long-term benefits of management techniques against short-term disadvantages for some species. Any kind of management is going to benefit some animals and plants and hurt others. The key is to be conscious of the impact of your decisions and balance your management actions in a thoughtful way over time.

Reptiles and Amphibians

While they are seldom seen and often ignored by prairie managers, reptiles and amphibians are important components of high-quality prairies. The following is a synthesis of management tips you can keep in mind as you devise annual and long-term plans. However, remember that there will always be conflicts between your objectives and the needs of some species.

First, maintain variability in habitat structure to provide microsites for thermal and moisture regulation, and keep brush and trees to a minimum to provide open habitat. Managing for diverse plant and insect communities will provide habitat variability and consistent food sources. Avoid excess traffic and uncontrolled livestock access around wetlands to prevent soil compaction and to protect water quality. Vegetation around and between wetlands provides protective cover and heat protection for many species and is important for those like turtles that nest in uplands.

Finally, ephemeral (temporary) wetlands are important for many reasons. The lack of permanent water prevents the establishment of fish populations, which are very efficient predators of amphibian eggs and larvae. Turning ephemeral wetlands into permanent fish ponds can decimate amphibian populations.

In many ways, invasive species have become the most serious threat that prairie managers have to deal with. Native tree and shrub species like eastern redcedar, smooth sumac, and green ash that used to exist in scattered patches on the landscape are now extremely abundant and can quickly invade small prairies. They have been joined by a host of exotic species brought in purposefully and accidentally. Those species include woody plants, grasses, and forbs, and they have changed the complexion and composition of prairies forever. Intensive agricultural and industrial practices have also dramatically increased nitrogen deposition across the central part of the United States, essentially fertilizing prairies enough to increase productivity by around 10 percent or more. While this may sound relatively benign or even beneficial, additional productivity generally favors grasses, especially exotics, at the expense of native forbs and overall biodiversity.

Most of the time, the encroachment of invasive species can be minimized with a management plan that maximizes biodiversity. But there are some invasives that will become a problem regardless of management system, and you will have to deal with them by developing strategies over and above your other management. This book is not designed to give you comprehensive control strategies for each potential invader in your prairie, but the appendix will provide some basic information on various control strategies, including manual control (cutting, mowing, digging, etc.), biocontrol (grazing, introduction of control insects, etc.), and herbicide techniques. There is also a list of resources that can help you diagnose, prioritize, attack, and evaluate your success in controlling invaders.

Invasive Grasses

The vast majority of invasive grasses are cool-season nonnatives that were introduced for livestock forage, soil stabilization, or horticultural reasons. One major threat from these species is that they start to grow earlier in the season than most native grasses and forbs. Because of this, they gain a competitive advantage and often monopolize light and soil moisture before natives have even emerged from winter dormancy. In drought years, they typically gain an even bigger advantage because what rain does fall tends to come mainly in the spring. In addition, while some cool-season exotics do have high forage value, that value drops off quickly after they flower—usually in April and May. Some of the worst cool-season exotic grass invaders are smooth brome, Kentucky bluegrass, tall fescue, tall wheatgrass, intermediate wheatgrass, quackgrass, cheatgrass/Japanese brome, reed canarygrass (a native plant with a hybridized or nonnative strain that is invasive), and creeping meadow foxtail.

With cool-season invasive grasses, it is sometimes possible to take advantage of their early spring and late fall growth periods, targeting them while having less impact on native species. This is particularly true in southern prairies where a higher proportion of native plants are warm-season species. As discussed earlier, fire and grazing during the growing period of cool-season grasses can help suppress their growth, especially when the site is rested afterwards to allow competitors to recover. In severe cases, herbicide treatments in the early spring or late fall can be used when very few plants are growing other than these invasive grasses. But that should be used only in cases where there are very few susceptible native plants or when the situation is so dire that there are no other good options.

There are fewer warm-season invasive grasses than there are cool-season species, but they can be equally threatening to prairies and often much more difficult to control. Perhaps the worst is Caucasian, or old world, bluestem. As its name implies, it is closely related to big bluestem and little bluestem,

A technician stands on the boundary between prairie that was burned in the late spring (left) and is dominated by tall, warm-season native grasses, and prairie that was not hayed the previous summer (right) and is dominated by cool-season grasses such as redtop.

two very common native plants. Unfortunately, it also matches them closely in growth habits as well. That makes it very hard to control without having a simultaneous impact on native warm-season grasses. Other invasive warm-season grasses include Johnsongrass and Bermudagrass. The trick to successful control of all these species is to eradicate them while they are still in small patches (less than one-half acre or so). Spraying the entire patch with herbicide is often the most effective method, and followup spraying will be required. This method usually kills most of the vegetation in the sprayed patch, but that loss is preferable to the invasion and eventual loss of the entire prairie.

INVASIVE SPECIES

Invasive Forbs

Unfortunately, there are way too many examples of invasive forbs in prairies to list them here. Some of the worst are leafy spurge, sericea lespedeza, and Canada thistle. For some, like leafy spurge and purple loosestrife, biocontrol insects are beginning to provide successful control in some places, either eliminating the plant or reducing its abundance to nonthreatening levels. For others, like musk thistle, successful control often starts with eliminating seed sources and increasing the vigor of the native grassland vegetation. But there are countless others for which a variety of control strategies are needed, and vigilance can be the key to preventing their initial invasion or their return after control measures are implemented.

Invasive Trees

There is a constant tension between open prairie and woodland. Whether a particular tree is invasive or not sometimes depends on what your objective for the site is. If you are managing for open prairie, any tree can be an invader if it's moving into a place where you don't want it. In other situations, scattered oak trees, for example, can be a natural and important component of a prairie or savanna ecosystem.

As native and planted woodlands expand around the Midwest, the sources of seed for invasions are increasing dramatically, and trees are moving much more quickly into the remaining prairies. This is apparently overwhelming some of the natural controls on tree encroachment, including browsing animals, climate, and even prescribed fire. More-aggressive actions, especially in smaller prairies, are now needed to fend off invasion. This includes the use of herbicides to kill deciduous trees that would otherwise survive multiple fires and/or mowing treatments.

A number of native tree and shrub species can be invasive, especially when prairies are small and easily overtaken by aggressive woody plants.

Like most deciduous trees, this young cottonwood can resprout from the base following a prescribed fire. This ability to survive being cut off and/or burned makes deciduous trees and shrubs difficult to contain when they invade prairies.

When invasive trees become abundant enough, it takes substantial (and expensive) efforts to remove them. Constant preventative actions are much more efficient.

Eastern redcedar is the most widely distributed and serious invader in prairies throughout much of central North America. Historically controlled by fires, it has now been released from that control where fire is not often used as a management tool, and it can spread quickly by its bird-eaten berries. Very few animals like to eat the plant itself, so it tends to spread unhindered unless land managers actively stop it with fire, cutting, or other measures. Fortunately, it is one of the easiest trees to kill. A fire that scorches or burns all the needles, especially during the dormant season, will typically kill a tree, and it does not resprout after being cut down as many other trees do.

There are numerous other native trees and shrubs that can be problems in prairies, including almost any species but those that require shady habitats. A list of the more common native invaders includes honey locust, black locust, black cherry, persimmon, smooth sumac, rough-leaved dogwood, green ash, cottonwood, sandbar willow, and desert false indigo.

Besides increasingly abundant native trees, there are a number of nonnative trees and shrubs that are also invasive. Many of these were, ironically, introduced to the United States for their wildlife habitat benefits. Some of the more common invasive nonnatives are osage orange (native only to southern prairies), white mulberry, Siberian elm, Russian olive, autumn olive, honeysuckle species, and common, or European, buckthorn.

These deciduous trees and shrubs, both native and nonnative, almost always require herbicide treatment to fully control their spread, and the appendix has specific information on chemical control options. Cutting, mowing, and grazing can all help suppress them too, and with enough repetition may eventually kill them, but with much less success than herbicides. However, defoliation treatments can be made more effective by careful timing. Trees and shrubs are at their most vulnerable right after they leaf out in the spring because they are using up energy reserves from their roots to make leaves, but have not yet begun to replenish those reserves with photosynthesis. Repeatedly cutting them at this critical time over multiple years is the most likely nonchemical method to succeed.

Prioritizing Invasive Plant Species

Good planning is essential for successful invasive species control. It's not possible to attack everything at once, so it's critical to prioritize. The Nature Conservancy has developed a helpful way of prioritizing invasive problems. It is based on four categories: (A) current extent of the species on or near the site; (B) current and potential impact of the species; (C) value of the habitats/areas that the species infests or may infest; and (D) difficulty of control. Within each category, you can give each invasive species a score, if you like, or you can just use the categories to help you think about them in terms of their relative priority (figure 10). If you rank each species by category, you can then combine the scores across the categories to see what comes out as your highest priority. In category A, higher priority is given to species that are either not yet on the site or are just getting established. The idea is that you should prevent future problems before you deal with invasive species that are already entrenched. Large infestations that are still expanding should be dealt with before infestations that have essentially gone everywhere they can, but preventing new weeds from becoming a problem should always come first. In other words, you should first spend your time patrolling the edges of your prairie to spot-spray any leafy spurge moving in from a neighbor's place. And then, if you have time left over, you can start working on the Kentucky bluegrass that invaded the site completely back in the 1930s.

When considering the impact of an invasive species (category B), think about how the species is altering, or could alter, the prairie community if it becomes established. For example, species that could completely prevent you from burning (like trees or shrubs that prevent grass growth underneath them) should get top priority. Next, invasive plants that can outcompete or displace native plants even under good management (like old world bluestem) should get higher priority than species that only invade places where the vegetation has been severely weakened. So take out the cedar trees that will prevent grassland bird nesting and make burning difficult before you worry about the sow thistle that is popping up around a windmill.

The third category (C) asks you to think about the value of the habitat the species could infest. Only you can decide which parts of your property are the most valuable. They could be the areas you think are the most attractive, the most diverse, or just the ones that are easiest to see from the house or the road. Concentrate on the species that are threatening the most important parts of your property first.

The final category (D) is difficulty of control. Essentially, you need to decide how good your chances are of eliminating or controlling each of the invasive species you have to deal with. The species for which you have the equipment, money, time, and ability to control should get a higher priority than those that you probably can't afford to control, or those that would just evade your best efforts regardless of how much time, money, and technology you throw at them. This is the time for you to think about whether you're wasting a lot of time on a battle you can't win while ignoring others that you could.

	Categories for evaluation				
	A	B	C	D	Total
Weed a	3	2	2	3	10
Weed b	1	2	1	2	6
Weed c	2	2	1	2	7

Establishing priorities for invasive species control: Categories for evaluation, ranked from highest to lowest priority. Weed species with lowest scores receive highest priority.

A. Extent of invasion
    1. Invasive species is present only on nearby sites.
    2. New populations are present.
    3. Large infestation is still expanding.
    4. Large infestation is no longer expanding.

B. Impact of invader
    1. Species alters ecosystem processes.
    2. Species outcompetes native species.
    3. Species does not outcompete natives but has other impacts.
    4. Species can exclude natives only after rare severe events (floods, tillage, etc.).

C. Value of infested area
    1. Infestation is in high-quality area with important or rare species.
    2. Infestation is in lower-quality area.

D. Difficulty of control
    1. Species is likely to be controlled and be replaced by natives.
    2. Species is likely to be controlled but will require restoration.
    3. Species is difficult to control, and control efforts will severely damage natural communities.
    4. Species is unlikely to be controlled with available resources/technology.

Figure 10. An example of how to rank species using a simple matrix. Species with low total scores should have higher priority than those with high scores. In the above example, weed B is not yet on the site, outcompetes native species, is likely to infest high-quality sites, and can be controlled. It is given higher priority than weed A, which is already well established on the site and will be difficult to control without damaging the natural communities on the site. Of course, any invasive species that outcompetes native vegetation should be controlled if possible, but this allows prioritization when time and resources are limited.

In this photo, weedy species like western ragweed, velvety gaura, and foxtail barley are abundant. However, all three species respond well to intensive grazing treatments but quickly give way to dominant grasses and other prairie plants as the prairie is rested. These plant species typically do not require herbicide application or any other treatment other than rest from grazing to allow recovery by other plants.

Overall, it's important to set ambitious but reasonable goals for controlling invasives. Make sure your goals are linked to the objectives you have for your property. State noxious-weed laws will require that you control some species of weeds, but most weeds or invasive animals are problems only so far as they conflict with what you want. If an invasive species can be eliminated from your property, that's the best long-term solution, but for many species that's not a reasonable goal. Try to figure out what kind of abundance might be acceptable, or on which parts of the property you could live with some level of infestation.

As an example, Kentucky bluegrass is a species for which eradication is rarely feasible. However, it is a species that often conflicts with the objective of maintaining a diverse plant community, especially in western prairies. A reasonable goal might be to eliminate it from some of the really high-quality portions of the prairie, where you're willing to spend time hand-spraying small patches that are trying to invade. But you might decide that it's always going to be a part of the rest of the property, and that you'll try to reduce its vigor once every third year or so with fire or grazing. If you want to measure your progress, you can try to estimate its dominance in a few specific places (e.g., 60 percent ground cover) and set long-term goals to reduce that (e.g., 40 percent ground cover). That way you can see whether or not the strategies you're using are working.

Taking Action

Once again, this book is not designed to provide the best answer for dealing with every conceivable invasive species. There is a wealth of information available for most species, and the appendix will guide you to that and provide you with technical advice on herbicides, equipment, and strategies. However, be aware that the battle landscape is constantly changing. With invasive plants, for example, new herbicides are always being introduced, and weeds can develop resistance to older herbicides over time. It's always a good idea to find the most current recommendations available, and to check with other people who are dealing with the same invasive species you're fighting.

There is, however, a general approach to attacking invasive plants that is applicable to almost every situation. It's often tempting to jump into the middle of a thick patch of weeds and start whacking or spraying everything in sight. When you're through, you can look at what you've done and feel good that you've taken a big bite out of the problem. Unfortunately, that's rarely the most efficient way to attack an infestation. Reducing the seed set or dispersal from the largest patches by mowing the flowers off or knocking the plants down can certainly be helpful in catching up to a big problem, but, often, control should start at the edges.

Sometimes, an invasive plant spreads in concentric circles around an initial invasion point, but other times it marches across the prairie with a

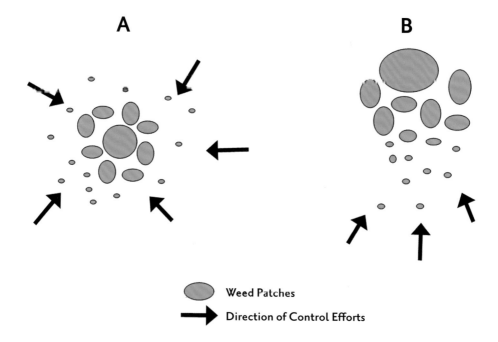

A

B

Weed Patches

Direction of Control Efforts

Figure 11. The recommended way to attack weed infestations. In example A, the weed seems to be spreading in all directions from a central source and the control strategy is to work from the edges toward the center. In example B, the weed is spreading in one direction and the control effort targets the leading edge first and then proceeds toward the source of the infestation. Controlling the smaller outer patches first contains the spread of the weed and ensures that new infestations are stopped before they become well established.

well-defined track (figure 11). Either way, there are a couple of advantages to starting your control at the edges of the infestation and working your way methodically toward the worst patches. First, you can protect the areas that haven't been affected yet while you try to recover the ones that have. Second, this method helps to contain the spread and reduce the eventual size of the infestation. Finally, it helps to keep you from feeling overwhelmed and giving up in disgust.

Most invasive plants will need repeated treatments over weeks, seasons, or years before they can be eradicated from a particular area of your site. Usually, the thickest, biggest patches take the most retreatments because they've been there the longest and they have either lots of seeds in the soil beneath them or well-developed root systems that take a while to kill (or both). If you can keep the new invasion areas from becoming that serious, you'll gain more than you might lose by waiting a while longer on the areas that are already about as bad as they can get. Above all else, be sure to stay on top of the areas you've already treated so that you don't lose ground there. If you can contain the spread effectively, you'll have the best chance to eliminate the weed from the site.

The "work from the edges" approach is effective both on the site scale (working to eliminate Canada thistle from your prairie) and on the weed-patch scale (working from the edge of each individual patch toward its center). On the site scale, your goal is elimination of the weed from your entire site, so you work the weed patches near the edges of the site or infestation first, and then move toward the more severe areas. When tackling individual patches of weeds within the site, it's helpful to apply the same strategy. This time, however, you're making sure you cover the outside edge of the patch well before moving to the center of it. In both cases, the overall purpose is to shrink the infestation toward its center or point of origin without letting it jump over your control lines along the way.

Using Herbicide

Infestations of most invasive plant species require some kind of herbicide application to eliminate them. Other control measures such as burning, grazing, mowing, or chopping can slow the infestation, weaken plants so that less herbicide is needed, or even reduce the total number of plants, but those measures are rarely sufficient on their own, even with many repetitions. Exceptions are species such as eastern redcedar and musk thistles, for which chopping and digging, respectively, can be very effective.

When herbicide application is necessary, there are some good ways to reduce its harmful impact on the biodiversity of your site. Be sure to pick herbicides that are as selective as possible and have the least possible residual effect, without compromising their effectiveness. For example, when spraying scattered individuals of a forb, it's not necessary to use a chemical like glyphosate (e.g., Roundup) which kills everything green. A chemical that acts only on broadleaf plants will reduce the number of nontarget plants killed, and sometimes options are available that kill only plants in a particular taxonomic family (legumes, for example). Some herbicides are designed to provide long-lasting control by preventing future seed germination as well as killing the current plants. Be sure that the prevention of seed germination is helpful to your cause if you choose that option. The germination-prevention action is usually universal, not restricted to the plant species you want to kill, so it may also inhibit the reestablishment of the native plants you need to compete with the invasives. In addition, some chemicals are slow to break down in the soil or water, and can cause long-term negative effects either by preventing or stunting future growth of vegetation where they've been sprayed, or by harming the health of other species, including animals. One of the advantages of glyphosate herbicides is that they affect only plants that are actively growing, and become inert once they bind with soil particles. This provides the option of spraying a weed that grows earlier or later in the season than most other plants (smooth brome or other cool-season grasses)—and you can avoid killing native plants that are dormant at the time. Regardless, killing more species or plants than you intend, either at the time of spraying or afterward, can be avoided by making good product choices. In addition to the impact on biodiversity, killing nontarget plant species can hurt your chances of controlling target plants if it prevents the surrounding native vegetation from filling in the empty space left by the dead weed plant.

Another way to reduce the harmful effects of herbicide use is to spray the smallest possible area around the target weeds. Spot-spraying, or spraying individual plants and patches of plants, is almost always the best option, compared to broadcast spraying. For extremely large infestations there may be absolutely no way to spray individual weeds or patches of weeds, so broadcast spraying (boom spraying from tractors, ATVs, aircraft, etc.) could be the only option. But even in those cases, it's possible to be somewhat selective. For example, if you have a Canada thistle infestation on 40 acres, it might be necessary to broadcast-spray 10 acres of the highest-density populations, but spot-spray on the other 30 acres. As with selectivity of herbicides, being selective about what areas get sprayed can benefit both the biodiversity of the site and the long-term success of the control effort. The more plants and species of plants that are left after a herbicide treatment, the greater the chance they will be able to outcompete the weed as it tries to make its comeback. Spot spraying might appear to be more time-intensive and expensive at first, but it can turn out to be the best option in the long run because of the increased vigor of the plant community.

Followup Visits

It is extremely important to revisit the site after any treatment of invasive species. First, you'll want to make sure you hit your target (did you miss any thistles?). If you missed, you can try again while the window of opportunity is still open. Second, you'll want to see whether your treatment had the desired effect (did the plants die, or just wilt a little and keep growing?). Third, you'll want to see whether there were resprouts or new plants that came up after your treatment (did the rain after you sprayed generate new seedlings?).

The timing of followup visits is also important. With herbicide treatments, you'll want to go back once after the plants start to show signs of wilting/browning so that you can see what you missed, but you should also go back again a week or two later to see if they actually died. Then you should make additional visits over the next months and years to look for resprouts or new plants. Regardless of the species being treated, the process of control will be a long one, so the purpose of following up and evaluating your success is to learn from your early attempts and design your next try to be even more successful.

Goats and Other Grazers as Weed Control

Goats and other grazers (cattle, sheep, etc.) can be useful as part of a weed control strategy. Repeated defoliation of plants over multiple seasons can weaken both their aboveground and belowground vigor. However, there are few if any well-documented cases of grazing animals eliminating a serious invasive plant infestation by themselves. More often, when a manager finally stops the grazing treatments, even after 5 or 10 years, the infestation return to pretreatment levels within a year or two. One major reason for this is that it's very difficult to keep grazing animals from switching to other plants once the target plant has been grazed short. This gives the weed time to recover and simultaneously reduces the vigor of the competing native vegetation. Careful herding of animals from weed patch to weed patch, and repetition of that treatment all season for several seasons has the best chance of success. But even under the best circumstances, grazing is almost always only part of a successful strategy. Grazing can be a way to suppress the vigor of plants and prevent seed set in a large infestation, while herbicide treatment is being used as the lethal control method.

In recent years, goat grazing has received attention as an innovative strategy for controlling brushy weeds such as eastern redcedar and others, as well as species like leafy spurge. Unfortunately, there has been very little research on the long-term benefits of this strategy, and its promotion has come mainly from the owners of goats. Be suspicious of those offering their grazing animals as the solution to your weed problem—especially if they expect you to pay for the right to have their animals on your land. Regardless of why you want their animals grazing on your land, you are still providing feed for those animals, and that value should be accounted for.

A Note on Feral Hogs

Feral hogs are an underrecognized serious threat to prairies and other natural areas, and they are spreading quickly across the Midwest. Technically, a feral hog is any pig that is roaming freely outside a pen or fence. Most feral hogs are escaped domestic hogs, Eurasian (Russian) wild boars, or a hybrid of the two. Some are simply hogs that have gotten out of pens or were released into the wild. Others are released for hunting purposes. Either way, they can cause very serious damage to both natural areas and cropfields.

The appearance of feral hogs can vary greatly, and depends upon both their genetic background and how long the population has been wild. Domestic hogs change dramatically in appearance within just a couple of generations upon becoming wild, growing longer hair and tusks, and changing color. Feral hogs can be black, white, brown, gray, or red, and are often a combination of colors. All of them can raise the hair on their back, giving them the look of a razorback.

Feral hogs use a variety of habitats, but generally like dense vegetation near water. Most of the damage they cause comes from rooting for food. They cause extensive soil disturbance and erosion problems, especially near streams and wetlands. They will eat almost anything, but generally eat grass and forbs in the spring and summer and nuts and roots in the fall and winter. Invertebrates (insects, earthworms, etc.) make up a significant part of their diet as well. However, they sometimes kill and eat larger animals, including calves and adult sheep and goats, and will feed on carrion when it is available. Because of this, their damage to wildlife species comes through competition for food resources, and also from killing and eating wildlife, including eggs and young.

Controlling a feral hog population is very difficult. Pigs are smarter than you think. It is nearly impossible to shoot every hog in a group at once, and if you try and fail, the surviving hogs will change their habits dramatically—even to the point of becoming nocturnal—to foil future attempts. It is critical to notify your state wildlife agency immediately if you suspect you have feral hogs in the neighborhood. Let the agency biologists decide the best course of action. If you try to handle the problem yourself, it is very likely that their job will be more difficult later. Often the best solution is to trap the entire population at once, which requires extensive experience and equipment.

prairie management

Sometimes a prairie is missing plant species, and not even top-notch prairie management can bring them back. If your prairie is near other prairies where those species exist, they may come back on their own. Otherwise, if the species are important enough, it might be necessary to bring seed in yourself to get them established. In more severe cases, you may have cropland, tame pasture, or some other complete conversion of a prairie to restore. There are other books besides this one that will provide comprehensive information on prairie restoration, particularly related to the reseeding of cropfields, and some of those are listed in the appendix. However, the following information can help to get you started.

Seed Sources

Establishing new plant species from seed is usually the best option. Transplanting mature plants from other sites can sometimes work as well, but that means that you are removing plants from somewhere else, which is usually not a good idea. A third option is to combine the first two options by obtaining seed and growing them into plants in a greenhouse and then transplanting those plugs. There are basically two ways to obtain seed; buy it or harvest it yourself. Either way you go, there are important guidelines that relate to the origin of the seed you obtain.

If you are adding plant species to an existing prairie or reseeding a cropfield near an existing prairie, you need to think carefully about the genetic implications. Bringing in new genetic material and allowing it to intermix with the genes of existing plants can carry risk, although the level of that risk is still poorly known. For example, let's say you live in eastern Minnesota and want to do a cropfield restoration project near a prairie. You can go to a nearby seed company and buy seed for a number of native grasses and wildflowers. However, you may not be able to learn the actual geographic origin of the seed you buy.

Taking one species, purple prairie clover, as an example, let's assume the seed you buy to plant in Minnesota was originally harvested from a prairie in central Kansas. When you plant seed with genetic material adapted to Kansas you are taking several risks. First, there is the risk that the plants will not be able to survive in eastern Minnesota. The climate and soils may both be very different from the conditions to which the Kansas prairie clover is adapted. Also, prairie clover in Kansas begins growing and blooming considerably earlier in the year than prairie clover in Minnesota. Yours might now bloom early enough that it misses important pollinators that haven't yet emerged, or even worse, it might begin growing so early that it gets killed in a late freeze.

The second risk of moving Kansas seed to Minnesota is that if it does survive, its pollen could spread to other prairie clover plants that are locally native to eastern Minnesota. If that happens, it's possible that the genetic information from Kansas could intermingle with that from Minnesota and create prairie clover plants that are no longer as well adapted to Minnesota conditions. Now, you may have hurt not only the prairie clover in your own prairie, but also decreased the chances of survival for the prairie clover that was already in the nearby landscape.

The data to support the level of risk from moving nonlocal seed into an area are still inconclusive, particularly on the issue of genetic pollution from outside sources. There are numerous examples of seed from faraway origins failing to survive under local conditions; that happens most often when seed is transported north or south. But whether or not nonlocal seed can pollute the genetics of local populations is still being hotly debated. The other possibility, of course, is that the added genetic information could actually strengthen the genetic diversity of the population and increase its fitness and resilience. However, it seems reasonable at this point to follow the safe route, and use seed obtained from sources as close to your planting site as possible.

Another risk you may encounter when buying seed is ending up with species that are not actually natives. A number of commercially available wildflower mixes contain species that are either nonnative or naturalized (naturalized generally means that a species is nonnative, but seems to be well adapted to a site). Many of these species have become invasive and are causing damage to natural areas. A few examples are dames rocket, oxeye daisy, and bird's-foot trefoil. Check with local biologists or literature to make sure that the species you're buying are truly native to your area.

Harvesting Seed

If you can't find a seed company that can sell you native seed with local origins, your other option is to harvest the seed yourself. Harvesting seed by hand can be a rewarding experience, and with a little practice you can get surprisingly large amounts relatively quickly. Once you've located plants to harvest (and have permission from the owner), the next challenge is to figure out when the seed is ripe enough. If you can find the actual seed, and not just the hull or pod that contains the seed, try to break or pinch the seed with your fingers. If the seed is milky or juicy inside it's too early to pick it, but if it's doughy or hard it's ready to go. Once you've harvested, lay the seeds out in a well-ventilated area to prevent them from becoming moldy while they dry. After they are completely dried, you may need to break the seeds apart from each other, out of pods, or off of stems, and you can do that with a hammer mill, a leaf shredder machine, or by hand. Then put them in a non-airtight container like a paper sack and store them in a cool dry place until it's time to plant.

Planting

When planting seeds, there are several important considerations. First, many seeds need to break dormancy before they can germinate. For many species that means a combination of cold and moist conditions over varying amounts of time. One way to help ensure that seeds will germinate quickly in the

Hand-harvesting of seed can be a quick and efficient way to obtain local-ecotype prairie seed for your restoration work. The most difficult parts of seed harvesting are identifying the plants and finding big patches of the species you want to harvest from.

spring is to plant them during the winter. This will allow them to go through any required cold stratification and to soak up moisture prior to germination. It can also give the seeds time to work their way into the soil during the freezing and thawing cycles of a long winter.

A second consideration is that the seeds will need contact with bare soil in order to germinate. When planting into a disked cropfield, this is not much of a problem, but planting into existing sod will require some kind of soil disturbance. Options include broadcasting seeds in areas of bare soil around badger mounds or gopher holes, planting after a fire, doing some light disking or

Pocket gopher mounds and disturbed soil from other burrowing animals can provide places for seed establishment in prairies, and can be taken advantage of when interseeding existing grasslands.

harrowing prior to broadcasting seeds, using cattle to trample the seeds into the soil, or using a no-till seed drill that puts the seed directly into the soil. Be careful not to plant the seeds too deeply, because many of them need light to germinate. Broadcasting seed right on top of the soil is often the most effective seeding method, and a light harrow or rake to just barely cover the seed can help increase seed-to-soil contact.

The third thing to consider is the competition for light and water that new seedlings will encounter as they germinate. In a former cropfield, the main competition will be annual weeds, and native prairie plants can generally out-compete them with little or no help from you. In cases where weed competition is so rank and tall that no light is hitting the ground, it may be necessary to mow or shred the weeds periodically—being careful not to mow off new seedlings in the process.

In prairie interseedings, suppressing competition from existing vegetation can be more difficult. In severe cases of cool-season grass infestations, an early spring or late fall herbicide treatment can open up space for seeds to establish, but disking or other technique may still be needed to get good seed-to-soil contact. In other cases, a heavy grazing treatment or growing-season fire in the season prior to planting can provide a good opportunity to add seed to a degraded prairie. Patch-burn grazing, or a similar fire/grazing combination, is another excellent way to provide for good seedling establishment, especially if seed is planted immediately after a fire. Besides the suppression of competing vegetation and exposure of soil by grazing, the hoof action of the cattle may also help to push the seeds into the soil. However, on the whole, the prairie restoration community is still struggling to devise consistently successful ways of seeding into established prairie communities.

Finally, be sure that the seeds being planted match the habitats you're trying to restore. Wetland seeds should obviously not be planted at the top of a hill, but there are more subtle factors that are important as well. Seeds harvested from sandy sites may not do well in rich soils (and vice versa). If you don't harvest the seeds yourself, find out as much as you can about the site(s) they were harvested from, and match conditions as closely as possible.

Prairie restoration through seeding can be an effective way to bring back plant diversity to a site, but it also needs careful thought. Be sure to get seed from native species with local origins. When harvesting seed, double-check to make sure that the plants you're harvesting actually have seeds in their pods and that the seed is ripe. Then consider how you're going to provide the conditions the seeds need to germinate and establish successfully. There are excellent resources on prairie restoration available in books and on the Internet, but you will get a lot of conflicting advice. Talking to local people who have had success in the same soil and weather conditions is often the best option. Finally, be patient. Even under good conditions it might take a couple of years to see the results of your work. And sometimes it takes 5 to 10 years to see anything come up from plantings, particularly when seeding into existing prairies.

Conclusion

Despite the seemingly mysterious and wonderful workings of prairies, they are not magical. Rather, prairies are incredibly complex and fascinating ecological systems that we don't completely understand. In that way they are similar to the human body. Interestingly, many of the same management concepts apply to both. Your cardiovascular system and all of the various muscle groups need to be alternately stressed and rested to achieve peak physical fitness. Likewise, a prairie has a diversity of species and communities with important roles to play in the function of the ecosystem. The fitness of the prairie depends on regularly exercising all of those parts.

Like effective physical fitness training, prairie management should vary in intensity and be nonrepetitive and adaptive. There is a wide array of tools available to manage prairies. Some, like grazing and fire, are historical disturbances that prairies have adapted to over thousands of years, but other, newer tools like herbicides and sickle-bar mowers can also be very useful. Having a variety of tools is important, but the real key is to use them in a purposeful, thoughtful way, responding to the needs of the prairie community.

The fragmented landscapes most prairies exist in today make management even more important. The grassland that existed before European settlement was like an expansive ocean in which plant and animal species alike could

float freely, allowing them to survive changing climate and other conditions. Today's small prairies are more like islands, and their species must rely only on the resources they can reach within their small range.

The future of fragmented prairies depends on their connectivity to other prairies. In some cases, restoration of the landscape between and around existing remnant prairies is the only real hope. But for many prairies, there are other grasslands and natural communities nearby to interact with. Looking across the fences and managing your prairie in the context of its surroundings are very important. If your prairie can provide missing habitat or resources for those other communities, the viability of the entire system increases.

The biggest threat to prairies, fragmented or not, is from invasive species. Small prairies are at greater risk because of their proportionally larger exposure to edges where invasions tend to start. But no prairie is large enough to be safe from an ever-growing array of plant and animal invaders. The greatest danger comes from those species that can completely alter the composition and function of a prairie. A sufficient density of trees, for example, can prevent grassland birds from nesting, shade out plant species, restrict the movement of wind-carried pollen, and even reduce the amount of grass fuel available for fires that might control the further expansion of the trees. Thoughtful and vigilant management is critical to help repel potential invaders, but even the best-managed prairies are vulnerable. The key to successful invasive-species control is to identify the threat early and suppress it before it becomes unmanageable.

Prairie management can be complicated and requires careful planning, but there is actually little risk of destroying your prairie by experimenting with new ideas. Prairies exist because of their resilience, and they can survive almost anything you throw at them. In fact, constant experimentation by prairie managers is critically important to the whole prairie conservation movement. The history of prairie conservation is still relatively brief, and even "experts" have much to learn about how to maintain the biological diversity of grasslands. You can contribute significantly to our collective wisdom by trying new things and documenting the results. Most important, be sure

Rainbow over loess hills prairie in Iowa at The Nature Conservancy's Broken Kettle Grasslands.

to step back periodically to admire your work and appreciate the beauty and complexity of your prairie. Take time to smell the wild roses, and take pride in your contribution to the conservation of one of the most fascinating natural communities in the world.

A Note on Climate Change

As the research continues to roll in on global warming and the resulting rapid climate change we will be experiencing in the next decades, you may wonder whether investing time and energy into prairie management is really worthwhile. This is obviously something I've struggled with as well, and my current opinion is that prairie management and restoration will be just as important in the future as it is now.

First, there are some good reasons to hope that prairies will be less directly affected by climate change than many other ecosystems around the world. Our prairies in the central United States are far enough away from the oceans, for example, that a dramatic rise in sea levels won't flood us out. In addition, there is a great deal of uncertainty in climate-predicting models right now, but the majority of what I've seen shows that prairies in this area will likely experience a less drastic change in climate than will landscapes in other areas. One likely scenario is that temperature and moisture extremes will intensify. Our summers will be hotter and our floods and droughts more extreme. These will be great challenges, to be sure, but prairies are tough and resilient and built for adapting to changing conditions.

It may be that the greatest challenge to prairies from climate change will be the more indirect effects, especially those caused by land use practices aimed at responding to climate change. Society is looking for alternatives to fossil fuels, which is good, but this search creates unintended consequences as well.

One of the most important of those relates to rowcrop agricultural practices. Even now, we are losing prairies at an accelerated rate because they are being converted to row crops for biofuels, especially corn ethanol and soy diesel. The long-term future of those industries is uncertain, but we will certainly see more prairies plowed up in the near term to feed our national appetite for fuel. Future farm policy will be extremely important in determining the future of grasslands in this country.

The second indirect threat to prairies from climate change responses comes from the acceleration of wind power development. Wind turbines can cause some direct mortality to birds and bats, but the much larger threat comes from their impact as agents of habitat fragmentation. There is growing research showing that grassland birds, particularly prairie grouse, avoid using areas up to a mile from wind turbines and other tall structures. This footprint is exacerbated by the necessary roads, transmission lines, and other developments that accompany wind farms and increase their habitat footprint. Wind power can and should be an important part of our strategy to reduce fossil fuel consumption, but the high overlap between the best potential sites for wind development and our largest remaining native grasslands makes appropriate siting of wind farms extremely important.

Assuming that your particular prairie will survive conversion to row crops or some other equally sudden death, the immediate question is whether impending climate change alters the way you need to think about prairie management. After a great deal of conversation with other prairie managers and ecologists, I think the answer is no. The best way to prepare a prairie for an uncertain climatic future is to build resilience, which is driven largely by biological diversity. This entire book has focused on that very issue. More drastic swings in weather conditions will mean that plant communities must be able to adapt quickly to very dry or very wet conditions. A diversity of species will provide them their best chance of success. Larger, more connected prairies also have a better chance at maintaining populations of both plants and animals under stressful conditions.

Invasive species would have continued to increase in importance regardless of climate, but climate change will likely accelerate both the number and intensity of invasions. Plant communities weakened by wild swings in weather conditions will be more vulnerable to invasion, and some invasive species are predicted to become more aggressive. In particular, there has been speculation that warm-season plants and vines may be the biggest beneficiaries of the future climate. Again, this doesn't really change the way you will need to manage your prairie since invasive species should already be a top priority.

One particular issue related to prairie management that is likely to get increased scrutiny is the use of prescribed fire. Because fire essentially converts vegetation to carbon and lifts it directly to the atmosphere, some people have already questioned the relative value of prairie fires. The key point to remember in this discussion, though, is the age of the carbon being released into the environment. The primary reason for human-induced global warming is the release of carbon from fossil fuels—carbon that has been stored deep in the earth for millions of years and is being newly added to the presentday atmosphere. In contrast, grassland fires release carbon, but only that which has very recently been sequestered by prairie plants; essentially they recycle a portion of that carbon back into the atmosphere. Most important, even under a frequent fire regime, grasslands store more carbon than they release.

Rapid climate change will be a big challenge for prairies and for those of us in charge of their care, but there's no reason to throw up our hands and quit. If nothing else, climate change gives us a reason to put even more focus on building the resilience of our prairies and doing everything we can to put them in a position to succeed—whatever the future might bring. In fact, a healthy, diverse prairie will be a strong contributor to the fight against global warming. Prairies are very effective at sequestering carbon and, in contrast to trees, which store most of their carbon in their trunks where it can be released when the tree dies, grasslands store the bulk of their carbon below ground. That belowground carbon will remain there unless it is released by future plowing. So take whatever personal steps you can to reduce your fossil fuel consumption, and convince as many others as you can to follow your lead. Then get back to the important business of managing your prairie. The world is depending on you!

appendices

appendices

This appendix provides more detailed information on what you'll need to set up a grazing operation. Many of the details are general because you'll need to ask local experts about developing stocking rates, finding lessees, and determining your fence and water needs. However, this quick guide should help you know what kinds of questions to ask.

Grazing Stocking Rate

The stocking rate of a pasture is a measure of grazing intensity. Stocking rate calculations can be confusing at first, and the decision on what stocking rate to start with can be tricky. Fortunately, there are people in your area available to help you. The Natural Resources Conservation Service (NRCS), a unit of the U.S. Department of Agriculture, has people with expertise who should be able to get you started. Biologists who work on private lands may have similar expertise. See the listing of potential contacts for your area in appendix 6. When asking for help on setting your initial stocking rate, be sure to explain clearly your objectives for the grazing. If you're trying to suppress smooth brome, your stocking rate will be much different than if you're trying to create some patchy vegetation structure. People who commonly advise landowners on grazing stocking rates are used to dealing with agricultural production objectives, so it will be critical for you to clarify whether you're aiming for plant diversity, habitat structure, or production. It's also important to remember that you'll be able to adjust your stocking rate after the first year if it appears to be too heavy or too light. It's highly unlikely that you'll do any permanent damage with a one-year stocking rate that's too high.

If you want to try calculating your own stocking rate, the following two paragraphs will help you. If not, just skip them and work with local experts to get started. Some people talk about stocking rate in terms of the number of cattle per acre, or the number of acres per head. However, a real stocking rate measure also includes the weight of the animals and the length of time they are in the pasture. The most widely used unit of measurement for stocking rates is the animal unit month (AUM). An AUM is the approximate amount of forage a 1,000-pound cow with a calf will eat in one month. The idea is to give you a somewhat quantitative way to estimate how many grazing animals you can support on your prairie. Smaller animals eat less, so your site can support more of them than it can larger animals. The time component of the equation is important too, because it allows you to consider putting more animals on the prairie if you're going to graze for a shorter time. There is still some inconsistency in how animal units are defined, but table A-1 uses some common definitions. Calves will change weight during the season, so estimate the weight of the animal unit by what you expect it to weigh in the middle of the grazing season.

If you were in the cattle business you would try to figure out how many AUMs (consumed forage) you could remove from your pasture each year without hurting your long-term production. For example, you might decide that the rainfall, soil type, and plant composition of your site would allow you to take 100 AUMs per year from the pasture. If you wanted to graze for 5 months, you would be able to graze 20 cows with calves, assuming the pair of them weighed about 1,000 pounds (100 ÷ 5). If the cow-calf pairs weighed 1,400 pounds (more typical) you would then be able to support about 14 pairs (100 ÷ 5 ÷ 1.4). You could then calculate the stocking rate of the pasture as AUMs per acre. For example, if there were 50 acres in the previous example, the sustainable stocking rate for your pasture would be 0.4 AUMs per acre (50 acres ÷ 20 AUMs). However, the appropriate stocking rate for your prairie will depend on your particular objectives and may vary by year as your objectives change.

Table A-1. Animal Unit Equivalents

The animal unit (AU) equivalents for several examples of livestock.

Type of animal	Weight in pounds	Animal unit equivalent
Cow, dry (no calf)	1,000	0.92
Cow, with calf	1,000	1.00
Cow, with calf	1,400	1.40
Bull, mature	1,350	1.5
Yearling	800	0.80

Adapted from Nebraska Cooperative Extension Bulletin EC 86-113-C. "A Guide for Planning and Analyzing a Year-Round Forage Program."

Keeping a written record of each year's stocking rate, the weather that season, and the results you saw from the grazing will be very helpful over time. Once you have some experience you'll be able to make adjustments up or down in cattle numbers or season length based on experience and weather. When you consider weather in adjusting stocking rates from year to year, base your decisions on what the weather was like in the past year, not the year to come. We don't yet forecast long-term weather well enough to predict what the coming season will bring for rain, but you do know what the previous season was like. If it was dry last year, you may need to reduce your stocking rate to allow the prairie to recover a little. If it was exceedingly wet, you might increase the stocking rate to catch up with the vigor of the grass. However, the biggest driver for adjusting your stocking rate is the objective you have for the coming season's grazing treatments.

Infrastructure Needs for Grazing

Grazing a prairie requires some infrastructure that other management treatments don't. The bare necessities are a perimeter fence and some kind of livestock watering facility. There are a number of options for fence, but the two most common types are barbed-wire and smooth-wire electric. If you're going to be grazing your prairie with cattle over multiple years, it's probably worth investing in a good four-wire barbed-wire fence. In Nebraska, the price to have a contractor build that kind of fence is about $1.50 a foot at the time of this writing.

If you plan to use cattle infrequently or in different places each year, you may be able to get away with a temporary electric fence. A one-wire electric fence is sufficient for some places, but if you are near a heavily traveled road or are concerned about the ramifications of cows getting out, two wires are safer. Deer and other passersby may knock the fence down periodically, especially in the first several weeks after it is put up, so be prepared to check the fence daily, especially early in the season. If you have a good perimeter fence but want to split the pasture for a rotational system, a single-wire electric fence may be the best option, because you can change its location each year and the cost is low. There are several options for providing electricity to the fence, including 12-volt batteries, solar panels, or hard-wired electricity, and you can buy a fence charger that will use each of those options. Your lessee may be able to provide the electric fence and the charger as part of the lease arrangement.

There are several of options for providing water to your livestock. If you're experimenting with grazing on a short-term basis it's possible that you can get your lessee to provide water (by hauling it in daily, for example), but if you are putting in a permanent grazing system you'll want a permanent water source. You'll need local expertise on this because options vary widely depending upon groundwater depth, availability of streams or ponds, and other water sources. Often the best sources of advice on installing a water system include local well-drillers and county extension agents.

In general it's best to avoid using a pond or stream as a water source because cattle can be hard on either over time and neither may be dependable during droughts. If you do use natural water sources, there are ways to provide limited access to them and avoid some of the negative impact. You can get guidance on this from local experts at the NRCS or another federal or state agency. They may also be able to provide you with cost-share options on both fence and water installation. Multiple water source options can be helpful if your pasture is large, because you can turn them on or off to shift grazing intensity around and to prevent excessive grazing around any one place.

Lease Arrangements

Unless you own cattle, you will have to come up with some kind of lease arrangement if you are going to graze your prairie. You may be surprised at the level of demand for grass among cattle owners. If you advertise in the local paper or agricultural publication that you have a pasture to lease, it's likely you'll get quite a few interested people. While you may be happy just to find someone willing to bring his/her cattle to your property, be selective, and remember that the cattle owner sees this as a business transaction. Don't give away the value of your grass. Find out from a local extension agent or from other landowners what the lease rates are in the neighborhood before you begin negotiating. Specify exactly how many cattle you want and when and where they should be in the pasture. Use a written lease so that you both will have a copy of the agreement you make. Your extension agent may have templates of grazing leases you could use to start from.

If you're only asking for a short-term grazing period, you may be able to work out a deal where the lessee will provide electric fence and livestock water in return for a break on the lease rate. If you're expecting to graze for many years, the lessee may be willing to build a permanent fence for you in return for a bigger break on the lease. When both fence and water are already installed, it's fairly typical that the lessee will do annual maintenance (repairs up to a couple hundred dollars or so) but that the owner of the pasture will pay for major repairs and replacements. You might be able to work out an arrangement by which the lessee will fix the fence each year but you will provide the supplies. Often the lessee is also responsible for some control of invasive species, especially with those like musk thistles or eastern redcedar trees that just need to be cut or dug out. Anything more complicated may be better left in your own capable hands, but you can ask the lessee to help keep an eye out for invasives.

Appendix 2. Additional Information on Prescribed Fire

Prescribed fire is a difficult topic to address because in most places there are few easy options for getting your prairie burned. There are enough safety concerns with fire that if you don't have considerable experience it's not a good idea to try to burn your own site. Check with local conservation organizations to see if there are training courses offered in your area and volunteer yourself to help with other burns to gain experience. Other options can include experienced neighbors, contractors, local rural fire departments, or local conservation organizations. In all cases, the first step is to learn what your local laws concerning prescribed fire are. Talk to your local fire department, and find out what the protocol is for obtaining permission to burn. If you don't feel comfortable with burning your prairie yourself, check with your fire chief and/or other landowners in the area for other options. In some places, there are local contractors who can burn your prairie for you. Even local volunteer fire departments can sometimes help out, for a fee or just for experience.

There are three main steps to conducting a safe and effective burn on your prairie: planning, site preparation, and implementation.

Planning

The first step in planning a burn is to have a clear objective. Are you trying simply to remove the litter and standing dead grass? Are you trying to kill trees? If so, do you have large trees you want to save or do you want every-thing dead? Are you trying to suppress cool-season grasses or facilitate their growth? All of these questions should be answered before you start thinking about how and when the burn will be conducted.

Once you have an objective, there are at least five critical components to a fire plan. These are presented to give you an idea of the kind of planning that has to occur. Much more thought and information will be required to put to-gether an actual plan.

1. FIREBREAKS. Decide where you will stop the fire on all sides of the unit and what preparation you will need to make that happen. Roads, disked cropfields, and other bare areas can be helpful, but often you will want to use mowed lines or other kinds of breaks as well. If you mow a firebreak, make sure that you also rake the dead grass out before lighting the fire. If you're going to burn in the spring, mowing in the late fall can allow any cut grass that isn't raked out to settle down to the ground during the winter, where it will be much less likely to catch fire during your burn.

2. FUEL. Consider the kinds of fuels available within the unit to be burned and in the adjacent areas. Is the grass tall and continuous or short and patchy? Are there living trees or piles of dead trees that will shoot embers into the air when they're burned? What are the fuels outside the unit? Would you be able to easily catch a fire that hops over your line?

3. POTENTIAL HAZARDS. Are there buildings, fields, hay bales, or anything else inside the unit or downwind that could be vulnerable to fire? What kinds of concerns might there be with smoke from your fire? Are there homes or roads that would be affected by large amounts of smoke? Is your entire unit accessible by the equipment you plan to use for your fire? What about accessibility to adjacent sites?

4. DESIRED WEATHER CONDITIONS. A good weather forecast is essential. There are great websites (the National Weather Service and Weather Underground provide two of them) that give detailed forecasts of mul-

tiple conditions. In addition, you may be able to call your local National Weather Service office and talk to the public forecaster on the day of the fire to double-check conditions. Try to get forecasts that break down the day into hourly segments if possible, so you can get a feel for how the day will likely progress.

The air temperature, relative humidity, and wind speed will be the three biggest factors controlling your fire, but others are important too, like the atmospheric mixing height that helps determine how your smoke lifts. Generally speaking you'll want your air temperature to be between about 40 and 70 degrees Fahrenheit. When it's colder than that you can have trouble getting the fire to burn well, and you may experience problems with the functioning of both people and equipment. Higher temperatures will mean hotter fires, which can be both good and bad, and you don't want to burn in temperatures so hot that you risk heat exhaustion for crew members. The relative humidity is very important and should be between 30 and 60 percent for most fires. Lower than 30 percent can be dangerous in tallgrass vegetation, and higher than 60 percent can make it difficult for the fire to carry. Wind speeds of 10–15 mph are ideal, but a little higher wind speed can be acceptable in some circumstances. Lower wind speeds can actually be dangerous because the fire takes longer (more time for things to go wrong) and the wind is more likely to switch directions. Higher wind speeds are obviously trouble too, especially when you have a lot of fuel (tall, dense grass) and/or low humidity. Of equal importance to the wind speed is the wind direction. Be sure the wind is blowing in the direction you want and not toward any hazard areas. Double-check the forecast before lighting to make sure there is no potential for the wind to shift during the next 6–8 hours.

Finally, it is important to remember that the temperature, humidity, and wind must be considered as a group, not individually. A higher wind speed might be acceptable when relative humidity is high, for example, but not when it's already near the low end of the acceptable range. Don't burn near the low point of the relative-humidity range and the high point of the temperature and/or wind speed range.

5. CONTINGENCY PLANS. This is the most important but often least considered part of a good burn plan. Consider the worst-case scenario, and be ready for it. Do you have the equipment you need to catch a fire that escapes? Can you get that equipment where it needs to go? Do you know whom to call for help if the fire escapes? Who will watch the fire inside the unit while others are chasing the part that is escaping? What will you do if someone is injured during the fire? What happens if the water truck breaks down? Experienced prescribed-fire leaders commonly say, "If you haven't lost a fire, you will." Be sure that an escape is manageable and won't become a disaster.

A final, important component of planning is adequate equipment and crew to carry out the fire. The number of people you need will depend greatly on the size of the fire, the amount of fuel, the topography, the equipment you have, and the experience of the crew. It is difficult to conduct even a simple fire safely with fewer than 5 people, and 6 to 8 or more is often much better.

Some of the basic equipment needs for a fire include radios for communication, drip torches for lighting, portable water pumps, and safety equipment. Be sure to have a backup for each piece of equipment that you rely on. There are a number of water pump options, including backpack sprayers, ATV-mounted sprayers, and larger units that fit in the back of a truck or tractor or on a trailer. It is a good idea to have at least one or two larger units that have a high-pressure, low-volume pump. For the safety of your crew, it's important to have everyone wear leather boots and clothing without any nylon or other materials that could melt. Nomex, or some other kind of flame-retardant outerwear, is important as well. The specific equipment needs for your fire should be discussed with someone with lots of local experience burning your kind of site.

Site Preparation

Site preparation starts months before you light a fire because the first component of that preparation is determining that there is adequate fuel. If you graze or hay your prairie, make sure that there is enough regrowth available to carry a fire next season. In general you should plan for at least half a season of rest to build up sufficient thatch and dead material. If you plan to burn in the growing season (late spring or summer) you'll want even more fuel to carry the fire through the green, juicy vegetation.

Besides preparing your fuel, be sure your firebreaks are ready. If you are mowing breaks through tall fuel, they should be plenty wide and raked clean, with no tree piles, tall weedy areas, or cedar trees near the edge of the fire unit that could send embers across the firebreak in a strong gust. You may want to till or disk a line along the edge of a firebreak to expose mineral soil and make the fire easier to control. However, this kind of soil disturbance can have other serious consequences so consider your options carefully. Disked breaks can be an easy place for invasive plant species to gain a foothold. They can also affect many wildlife species, particularly turtles that like to nest in previously disked breaks and then are killed when the break is disked again.

Implementation

There are several ways to conduct a safe and effective prescribed fire. I will describe the most commonly used technique here, the ring fire approach, because it works well in many situations. It should definitely not be seen as the best or only method to burn a prairie, but it includes many of the important elements of a safely conducted fire.

With a ring fire, the ignition begins at the furthest downwind point of the burn unit (figure 12). The first step is to light the backing fire along the entire downwind edge of the firebreak, allowing the fire to back into the unit (against the wind) but not across the firebreak. The backing fire leaves behind a large swath of black burned area along that whole side. Then both flanks of the fire are lit (walking into the wind) simultaneously, and that fire is allowed to burn into the unit (sideways to the wind) but not across the firebreak. Once the flanks are sufficiently blackened, the head fire is lit across the upwind side of the fire and allowed to roar with the wind until it puts itself out when it hits the blackened border you created with the backing and flank fires.

Insurance and Liability

Every state deals differently with liability for prescribed fire. Check with an attorney or your insurance company to clarify your situation before you burn.

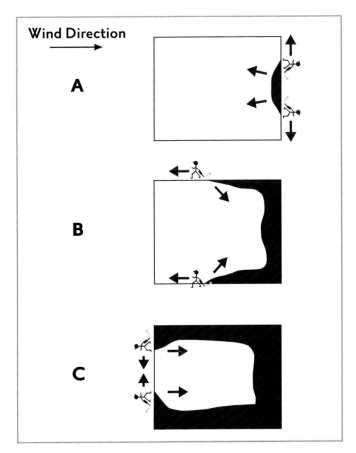

Wind Direction

A

B

C

Figure 12. A ring fire lighting pattern. In frame A, two igniters light a backing fire that is allowed to back into the wind. In frame B, the igniters are walking into the wind, igniting a flanking fire. In frame C, the igniters complete the ring and light a head fire that burns with the wind until it hits the already blackened areas and goes out.

In many cases prescribed fire is covered by the insurance held by agricultural landowners, but you should double-check your own situation. If you hire a contractor or someone else to burn your prairie, be sure you know who would be liable if something went wrong. Liability has to be taken very seriously these days. It should not necessarily stop you from burning, but it should definitely factor into your decision-making process.

appendices

There are many ways to attack invasive plant species, and the earlier chapter on invasives discussed most of them. Below are some further details on a few methods. Please note that herbicide recommendations are based on chemicals and herbicide brands available at the time this book was written. Herbicide availability changes frequently, as does the best advice on which ones to use in various situations. Brand names are used below as examples, but there are often multiple herbicide brands with the same chemical makeup, especially with active ingredients that have been available for a while. Check with someone you trust locally to find out what the most current options are for the weeds you're dealing with at your site. Please follow the label instructions on the herbicides. If anything on the label contradicts the advice given here, follow the label.

Trees

Eastern redcedar trees are a serious threat to prairies, but at least they're relatively easy to kill. Cutting them off below the bottom branch is usually sufficient to prevent any regrowth. Most other tree and shrub species, though, require the use of herbicides to ensure a good kill. Even cutting most deciduous trees down repeatedly is rarely successful, especially with young trees.

There are several options for effective herbicide application, including the cut-stump method, the streamline basal treatment, and the foliar application method.

Cut-stump Herbicide Application

The most efficient and ecologically friendly way to kill invasive trees is simply to cut them off and paint the stem with a relatively high concentration of herbicide. The concentration you need to use will depend upon the brand name. Use the least you can that will do the job. On small trees you should paint, spray, or dribble herbicide onto the entire top of the stump, but on larger trees, you usually need to hit only the outside 2–4 inches all the way around. The center, or heartwood, of large trees is used only for structural strength, not for transporting liquids up and down the tree. An old dishwashing-liquid container can be a good way to apply the chemical without wastage.

A clean and easy way to apply herbicide to cut stumps of small trees is with the PVC herbicide wand invented by Jack McGowan-Stinski of The Nature Conservancy in Michigan. The wand is essentially a long, thin PVC pipe with a valve and sponge at the bottom. You can find detailed instructions for building a wand at www.invasive.org/gist/tools/wandinst.pdf or simply by searching the Internet with the keywords PVC and herbicide.

There are other ways to get herbicide into trees without cutting them all the way down. You can girdle the tree (cut through the outside 2–4 inches of the tree all the way around) and apply herbicide inside the cut, for example. There are also injection methods for getting the herbicide through the bark to the living part of the tree. There are occasions when these methods are useful, but unless the tree is really big, I usually prefer to just cut it down (or use the streamline basal treatment below). It's better from a grassland-bird habitat standpoint to cut the trees out of the prairie too.

Be aware that if you cut down a deciduous tree but allow it to begin regrowing it's often much harder to kill the tree later. The tree still has a large root system that you have to kill with herbicide, but there's not much surface area on the aboveground portion to spray or paint. It's unavoidable that you'll miss a few stumps when you're working with a lot of trees, but it's well worth your time to hit as many as possible the first time around. If you do have to go back and try to kill regrowth later, be sure to hit every single stem that's suckering out of the base with herbicide.

The Streamline Basal Treatment for Killing Small Trees

One of the more daunting challenges for prairie managers is an abundance of small tree seedlings moving into their prairie. A large scattered stand can be frustrating because mowing doesn't do anything but topkill them, and there are too many to make it feasible to paint the cut stems with herbicide. The best method I'm aware of for dealing with this situation is called the streamline basal or basal bark treatment. The method works well on small trees that are less than 3 inches in diameter and still have smooth bark (as opposed to the rough, scaly bark on older trees).

To kill the trees you mix a herbicide consisting of the chemical triclopyr (examples include Remedy and Pathfinder II) with diesel fuel or crop oil at a ratio of 3:1 oil to herbicide (no water is used). Then you spray a small amount on the base of the small tree, somewhere on the lower 12 inches. On trees with a diameter of about 2 inches or less, you need to spray only a 2–3 inch wide band on one side of the tree. If the tree is larger, you might need to make the band go all the way around the base. But either way, it takes only a small amount, and if you are very careful there is hardly any overspray at all. The oil in the mixture helps the herbicide penetrate the thin bark and go into the cambium layer, where it kills the tree. Diesel fuel works very well and is the cheapest option for the oil part of the mixture, but in wetlands or other sensitive areas it's better to use crop oil or an even more highly refined oil. When using one of the more refined oils, you should include a penetrant (examples include Access Penetrator or Cidekick) as 5–10 percent of the mixture to help the chemical get to the inside of the tree.

A small (1–3 gallons) hand sprayer or backpack sprayer works well for this because it doesn't take very much mix to kill an awful lot of trees. Cleanup is a little trickier than with most herbicides because of the oil, but dishwashing liquid works well. Be warned that this mix is hard on sprayers, whether you use diesel or one of the other oils. The oil eats away the rubber seals and gaskets and you may have to replace the sprayer more often than you're used to. We've started buying cheap hand sprayers for exclusive use with this mixture so that we don't ruin our nicer backpack sprayers. In addition, Chris Rundstrom—The Nature Conservancy's land steward in central Nebraska—has found that the PVC herbicide wand described earlier also works well for this method and avoids the damage to sprayers.

The method works extremely well for small trees in most circumstances. It's especially nice when killing thorny trees like osage orange or honey locust because you don't have to get very close. The only time we've really had trouble getting a good kill is when we're using the method on a large tree that was cut and has regrown multiple sucker stems. If we can spray each of the stems we can sometimes kill the tree, but it's hard to get enough chemical in the tree to kill it that way. Usually we resort to a foliar spray, using a different mix in water.

One of the best things about the streamline basal treatment is that you can use it any time of year, even in the dead of winter! In fact, winter is a great time to spray this way because what little overspray there is hits only the dormant leaves of the surrounding vegetation. It's also a nice way to spend those periodic warm winter days. Be warned, however, that trees sprayed during the winter will still green up in the spring for a couple weeks before they die. This is because the tree's "pipelines" aren't active in the winter, and the chemical doesn't get transported to the roots until the tree becomes active again in the spring. It's a little unnerving at first when you see the trees you sprayed starting to get nice green leaves, but after a while they will wilt and die very nicely.

Foliar Application of Herbicide

In some cases, applying herbicide to the leaves of trees and shrubs is the only feasible option. When doing so, it is obviously important to be as careful as possible to avoid spraying nontarget plants. It is also important to use herbicides that are as selective as possible and that harm as few other plant species as possible.

One method of applying herbicide to the leaves of trees and shrubs without spraying is the use of a wick applicator. This used to be a fairly common tool in rowcrop agriculture, especially on soybeans, and consisted of a long pipe with rope wicks hanging from it. The wicks were dragged along the top of the weeds, but above the crop, so that the chemical was applied only to the vegetation sticking up above the soybeans. The same mechanism can be used on trees and shrubs or any other weeds that are taller than the surrounding prairie vegetation. Various brands and designs of wick applicators are available, including some that are more effective than others at getting adequate herbicide quantities on the plants. One particularly effective design consists of a rotating carpeted cylinder—rather than a rope—that applies the herbicide. A version of this style of weed wiper is made by Agriweld Inc.

Exotic Grasses

In many cases, carefully timed fire, grazing, and/or mowing can suppress cool-season grasses and allow native vegetation to sustain itself. In more seriously degraded sites it may be necessary to take more drastic action. Herbicides with the chemical glyphosate (Roundup, etc.) can be effective at killing cool-season grasses in the early spring and late fall when the majority of native plants are dormant. However, there are several difficulties involved. First and foremost, not all the native plants will be dormant, and the ones that aren't tend to be the ones that could help to replace the exotic grasses. Because glyphosate kills any plant that is actively photosynthesizing, think carefully before jumping into this strategy. Second, to get effective control with glyphosate you need warm temperatures (at least 60–65 degrees F) on the day you spray and, with luck, the next day or two as well. Glyphosate must be absorbed by actively growing plants, and even cool-season grasses don't grow well in really cool temperatures. Third, because the plants need to be actively growing to be affected by the herbicide, the treatment doesn't work well in drought conditions (or floods!). Because of these factors, the chance of finding a suitable opportunity to spray these grasses effectively in the spring or fall is often slim.

There are some other chemicals available for killing grasses, some of which are more selective than glyphosate. One is sethoxydim, found in the herbicides Select and Poast. Sethoxydim doesn't affect nongrass plants, including sedges, so it can be useful in some situations. However, there are few perennial grasses included on the label, meaning that it has not been tested on those other species. It also is not labeled for use with grazing or haying. Finally, when used at the recommended rate for control of perennial grasses, it is very expensive.

Often, the best solution for controlling dominant exotic grasses is repeated grazing, burning, or mowing over a number of years. Obviously, repeating the same treatment every year will be detrimental to plant diversity, as discussed earlier, but you will have to judge the level of threat and respond accordingly. Defoliating the grasses repeatedly through the early part of the growing season, or a one-time defoliation as the plants are preparing to bloom, will be the most effective at weakening them. The objective for these kinds of treatments is not eradication, but suppression. The hope is to make the exotic grasses a smaller component of a diverse plant community.

Finally, one of the reasons cool-season exotic grasses do well in many places is an excess of available nitrogen in the soil. You may notice that your exotic grass problem seems to be worst in the bottoms of draws adjacent to cropfields or other places where nitrogen is running off of nearby areas. If so, addressing the source of the nitrogen can help tremendously. It may still take a long time to de-nitrify the soil, but at least you'll have a chance of breaking the cycle. Haying can be an effective tool for removing nitrogen from the soil because it cuts and removes the plant material (and the nitrogen contained in it) each year. Again, the detriments of haying were discussed earlier in this book, but in some circumstances it might be the best available option.

Other Invasives

As mentioned earlier, there are too many invasive plant species out there for this book to address them individually. Universities, chemical companies, and land managers are constantly experimenting and searching for novel treatments for most of the worst ones. Check with sources listed below or local people to find out what the current best options are for the weeds you're dealing with.

I benefited from a number of information sources while writing this book. These included peer-reviewed literature, other published literature, websites, and personal conversations. Because the field of prairie management is still relatively young, the best information available changes rapidly as new data come in and new techniques are tested. I tried to ensure that I was as up to date as possible by asking a large number of reviewers to assess portions of the book that matched their particular expertise.

Prairie Ecology Introduction; Plant Communities; The Role of Disturbance

Statistics on the loss of prairie of different types vary somewhat, but a standard source of information is the 1994 *BioScience* article by Fred Samson and Fritz Knopf. A more detailed breakdown of the same information can be found in a 1998 article they wrote with Wayne Ostlie and published in a Northern Prairie Wildlife Research Center publication. The history of fire in prairies is often debated and can be a tricky subject because no one was recording data on fire frequency several thousand years ago. However, Tom Bragg has nicely encapsulated fire and soils information in his chapter on the physical environment of grasslands in *The Changing Prairie*. Additional information on fire, soils, and the basic ecology of prairies can be found, among other places, in Cornelia Mutel's book *The Emerald Horizon*; Steve Pyne's *Fire in America*; and *Grassland Dynamics: Long Term Ecological Research in Tallgrass Prairie* by Alan Knapp and others, which summarizes research from Konza Prairie Research Natural Area in Kansas. Information on glaciation and geologic timeframes for prairie came from *The True Prairie Ecosystem* by Paul Risser and colleagues, as well as from a 1992 paper published by Richard Baker and others. Grazing comparisons between bison and cattle are summarized nicely in David Hartnett, Al Steuter, and Karen Hickman's chapter on native and introduced ungulates in *Ecology and Conservation of Great Plains Vertebrates*. Climate information as it relates to prairie type was pulled largely from a 2003 article by Stanley Changnon, Kenneth Kunkel, and Derek Winstanley in *Transactions of the Illinois State Academy of Science*. Much of the information in these chapters also comes from my personal experiences and conversations with colleagues, particularly Gerry Steinauer, the state botanist for the Nebraska Game and Parks Commission.

Animal Communities

Most of the insect statistics in this chapter were pulled from summarized information in a paper by Richard Redak. Several websites have excellent resources on invertebrates of all kinds and were useful as well, including Bugwise.net (Australian Museum) and the National Biological Information Infrastructure website. Information on the biomass of grasshoppers at Konza Prairie came from a 2006 *BioScience* paper on grasshopper control theories by David Branson, Tony Joern, and Gregory Sword. Gary Belovsky and Jennifer Slade's excellent paper on insect herbivory and plant production provided me with good background for that section. James Trager's online article on prairie ants was wonderful, and personal conversations with him were equally useful. Brenda Molano-Flores from the Illinois Natural History Survey has also been a great source of information for me. In addition, I've become active in insect research in the past several years, much of that in collaboration with Craig Allen (University of Nebraska–Lincoln) and others.

Jim Herkert, now with The Nature Conservancy in Illinois, is among the top researchers in the field of grassland birds and habitat fragmentation. Jim has numerous papers on the subject and was helpful to me when I was doing my graduate research on the same topic. I now enjoy the ability to call him up on business and see him at meetings periodically. A number of other researchers and papers have addressed this topic as well. Upland game bird information was fact-checked by Scott Taylor with the Nebraska Game and Parks Commission and Steve Clubine with the Missouri Department of Conservation.

Information on reptiles and amphibians was gleaned from several of sources, as well as personal knowledge, but the most useful site for both general information and management implications was that of Partners in Amphibian and Reptile Conservation. Small mammal information was gleaned from multiple sources, including Konza Prairie's webzine, website, and research, summarized in *Grassland Dynamics*. In addition, the Illinois State Museum's website had great general information on small mammals and many other topics associated with Midewin National Tallgrass Prairie. Clay Nielsen of Southern Illinois University graciously answered many of my questions regarding predation, deer populations, and other mammal information. Aldo Leopold's writings on the detriments of predator control are legendary, particularly on the topic of deer overpopulation on the Kaibab Plateau in Utah and elsewhere in the intermountain west. His *Sand County Almanac* is a constant source of information and inspiration to me and nearly every ecologist I know. Information on the ecology of fear related to wolves and their impact on ecosystems comes from multiple studies by William Ripple and Robert Beschta and their students, much of which is nicely summarized in their 2004 *BioScience* article.

The Importance of Diversity and Heterogeneity

Chapter 4 incorporates many basic tenets of ecology that I have soaked up through years of classes and personal experience. Any basic ecology textbook will provide background information on subjects such as species richness and evenness, habitat heterogeneity, etc. The concept of diverse plant communities resisting invasion has been tested experimentally by Dave Tilman and colleagues at the University of Minnesota. One of the most recent papers on the subject was published by Joe Fargione and Dave Tilman in 2005. I am collaborating on research testing the same idea on a larger scale than the small plots used by Tilman's group.

Landscape Context

As with chapter 4, much of chapter 5 describes the essential concepts of the field of landscape ecology. I became very familiar with these concepts during my graduate work on grassland birds and the way they are influenced by habitat patch size and shape. I now apply the same concepts daily in my work as a conservation biologist, trying to figure out how to build landscapes that support agricultural production but still retain viable populations of wildlife and plants.

The Adaptive Management Process

The range of plant species likely to be found in high-quality prairies was supported by an informal survey of botanists from states throughout the region this book covers. The basic process of adaptive management, based on setting good objectives and "closing the loop" with measures that feed back into adjusted objectives and strategies, is adapted from *Conservation by Design*, which is The Nature Conservancy's framework for conservation strategy. The same concept is used by other conservation agencies and organizations as well, and is really just a formalization of the learning process thoughtful people use in most aspects of their lives: running a company, raising children, or cooking a meal.

Guiding Principles for Designing Management Strategies; Examples of Management Systems

Most of chapters 7 and 8 comes from my own work restoring and managing prairies, as well as from the many colleagues with whom I trade ideas and share learning experiences. The specific information on the impact of defoliation on plants comes from a wealth of literature in the field of range science dating back to the 1950s, including an excellent 1959 paper (Oswalt et al.). Information on the responses of plants to fire was supplemented by the book *Grasslands Dynamics* by Alan Knapp and his colleagues at Kansas State University. The review I mentioned of the science supporting rotational grazing was published in 2008 by a large group of authors (Briske et al.). Patch-burn grazing is being intensively tested by several universities and organizations, including The Nature Conservancy, Missouri Department of Conservation, Kansas State University, Iowa State University, and others. The method dates back to the 1980s and 1990s when people like Al Steuter and Bob Hamilton with The Nature Conservancy were trying to find ways to manage bison herds on native prairies by incorporating historical fire patterns. Both Al and Bob have been very helpful to me as I've experimented with fire and grazing on the lands I manage. Today, Oklahoma State University is the recognized leader in patch-burn grazing research because of pioneering work done by Sam Fuhlendorf and David Engle, along with a number of graduate students. Their 2001 article in *BioScience* nicely lays out the core components of patch-burn grazing as well as its ecological underpinnings.

Managing for Wildlife with Particular Requirements

The information on management for animal species in chapter 9 came from the same sources listed above for chapter 3. I've enjoyed spirited discussions with Ron Panzer about remnant-dependent insects and prairies (and numerous other topics), and he has a nice website that summarizes many of his views. In addition, Joel Jorgensen with the Nebraska Game and Parks Commission correctly pushed me to include shrub-dependent species. Partners in Amphibian and Reptile Conservation (PARC) was a great source for tips on management for those species.

Invasive Species

I've spent much of my professional career scheming against invasive species. Again, most of the information in this chapter comes from my personal knowledge and that of my colleagues. Conversations with John Randall and others in The Nature Conservancy's Global Invasive Species Team formed the basis of most of what I wrote about strategies for attacking infestations and prioritizing invasives. Excellent guidance on those topics along with extensive background on most invasive species can be found at their website. Sam Wilson, with the Nebraska Game and Parks Commission, provided me with much of the information on feral hogs and their control.

Restoration

Prairie restoration has just recently begun to make the transition from an art to a science. My own experience with prairie restoration techniques began with tutoring by Bill Whitney with the Prairie Plains Resource Institute in the mid 1990s. The techniques used by Prairie Plains and those of us influenced by them are nicely summarized in *A Guide to Prairie and Wetland Restoration in Eastern Nebraska* by Gerry Steinauer and others. That guide can be downloaded for free from the Prairie Plains website or from www.PrairieNebraska.org. In addition to my personal experience with prairie restoration, I've been heavily involved in the Grassland Restoration Network, which links together sites across North America working on high-diversity restoration of landscape-scale sites. The cross-site learning that has come from that network has been invaluable to me.

Appendices

Stocking rate information for cattle can be found in a variety of sources. The University of Nebraska Extension Bulletin article by Steven Waller et al. I used presents one version. Prescribed fire information comes from the training and experience I've received as a prescribed fire leader for The Nature Conservancy. The Conservancy's fire program has excellent resources online at www.tncfire.org that can be helpful for people at any stage of experience. Steve Clubine with the Missouri Department of Conservation provided helpful additions to the sections on invasive tree control, both through his *Native Warm-Season Grass Newsletter* and through personal communications.

The following is a list of the publications and websites I used as references for the information presented in this book. This list corresponds with the bibliographic notes presented in appendix 4.

Australian Museum Online. 2005. "Bugwise." www.bugwise.net.

Baker, R. G., L. J. Maher, C. A. Chumbley, and K. L. Van Zant. 1992. "Patterns of Holocene Environmental Change in the Midwestern United States." *Quaternary Research* 37:379–389.

Belovsky, G. E., and J. B. Slade. 2000. "Insect Herbivory Accelerates Nutrient Cycling and Increases Plant Production." www.pnas.org/cgi/doi/10.1073/pnas.250483797.

Bragg, T. B. 1995. "Climate, Soils, and Fire: The Physical Environment of North American Grasslands." In *The Changing Prairie*, ed. K. H. Keeler and A. Joern, 49–81. Oxford: Oxford University Press.

Branson, D. H., A. Joern, and G. A. Sword. 2006. "Sustainable Management of Insect Herbivores in Grassland Ecosystems: New Perspectives in Grasshopper Control." *BioScience* 56:1–13.

Briske, D. D., J. D. Derner, J. R. Brown, S. D. Fuhlendorf, W. T. Teague, K. M. Havstad, R. L. Gillen, A. J. Ash, and W. D. Wilms. 2008. "Rotational Grazing on Rangelands: Reconciliation of Perception and Experimental Evidence." *Rangeland Ecology and Management* 61:3–117.

Caldwell, J. 2002. "Small Mammals Focus of Kaufmans' Research." *K-State Perspec-*

tives. Online. http://www.mediarelations.k-state.edu/WEB/News/Webzine/konza/smammals.html.

Changnon, S. A., K. E. Kunkel, and D. Winstanley. 2003. "Quantification of Climate Conditions Important to the Tall Grass Prairie." *Transactions of the Illinois State Academy of Science* 96:41–54.

Clubine, S. *Native Warm-Season Grass Newsletter*. Online. http://www.prairiesource.com.

Fargione, J. E., and D. Tilman. 2005. "Diversity Decreases Invasion via Both Sampling and Complementarity Effects." *Ecology Letters* 8:604–611.

Fuhlendorf, S. D., and D. M. Engle. 2001. "Restoring Heterogeneity on Rangelands: Ecosystem Management Based on Evolutionary Grazing Patterns." *BioScience* 51:625–632.

Hartnett, D. C., A. A. Steuter, and K. R. Hickman. 1997. "Comparative Ecology of Native and Introduced Ungulates." In *Ecology and Conservation of Great Plains Vertebrates*, ed. F. L. Knopf and F. B. Samson, 72–101. New York: Springer-Verlag.

Illinois State Museum. 2003. "Plants and Animals: Mammals." www.museum.state.il.us/exhibits/midewin/mammals.html.

Knapp, A. K., J. M. Briggs, and D. C. Hartnett, eds. 1998. *Grassland Dynamics: Long-Term Ecological Research in Tallgrass Prairie*. New York: Oxford University Press.

Leopold, A. 1949. *A Sand County Almanac, and Sketches Here and There*. New York: Oxford University Press.

Mutel, C. F. 2008. *The Emerald Horizon: The History of Nature in Iowa*. Iowa City: University of Iowa Press.

National Biological Information Infrastructure. 2008. www.pollinators.nbii.gov/portal/server.pt.

The Nature Conservancy. 1996. *Conservation by Design: A Framework for Mission Success*. www.nature.org/aboutus/howwework/cbd/.

The Nature Conservancy's Global Fire Initiative. 2008. www.tncfire.org.

The Nature Conservancy's Global Invasive Species Team. 2008. www.tncinvasives.ucdavis.edu.

NatureServe. 2008. www.natureserve.org.

Oswalt, D. L., A. R. Bertrand, and M. R. Teel. 1959. "Influence of Nitrogen Fertilization and Clipping on Grass Roots." *Proceedings of the Soil Science Society of America* 23:228–230.

Panzer, R., K. Gnaedinger, and G. Derkovitz. 2006. "The Conservative Prairie and Savanna Insects of the Chicago Wilderness Region." www.neiu.edu/~cwinsect/.

Partners in Amphibian and Reptile Conservation. 2004. www.parcplace.org/.

Pyne, S. J. 1982. *Fire in America: A Cultural History of Wildland and Rural Fire*. Princeton University Press.

Redak, R. A. 2000. "Arthropods and Multispecies Habitat Conservation Plans: Are We Missing Something?" *Environmental Management*, vol. 26, supplement 1: S97–S107.

Ripple, W. J., and R. L. Beschta. 2004. "Wolves and the Ecology of Fear: Can Predation Risk Structure Ecosystems?" *BioScience* 54:755–766.

Risser, P. G., E. C. Birney, H. D. Blocker, S. W. May, W. J. Parton, and J. A. Wiens. 1981. *The True Prairie Ecosystem*. US/IBP Synthesis Series 16. Stroudsburg, PA: Hutchinson Ross.

Samson, F. B., and F. L. Knopf. 1994. "Prairie Conservation in North America." *Bioscience* 44:418–421.

———, F. L. Knopf, and W. R. Ostlie. 1998. "Grasslands." In *Status and Trends of the Nation's Biological Resources*, vol. 2, ed. M. J. Mac, P. A. Opler, C. E. Puckett Haecker, and P. D. Doran, 437–472. Jamestown, ND: Northern Prairie Wildlife Research Center Online. www.npwrc.usgs.gov/resource/habitat/grlands/index.htm.

Steinauer, G., W. Whitney, K. Adams, M. Bullerman, and C. Helzer. 2003. *A Guide to Prairie and Wetland Restoration in Eastern Nebraska*. Prairie Plains Resource Institute/Nebraska Game and Parks Commission.

Trager, J. C. 1998. "An Introduction to Ants (*Formicidae*) of the Tallgrass Prairie." *Missouri Prairie Journal* 18:4–8. Jamestown, ND: Northern Prairie Wildlife Research Center Online. www.npwrc.usgs.gov/resource/insects/ants/index.htm.

United States Department of Agriculture. 2009. PLANTS Database online. www.plants.usda.gov/index.html.

Waller, S. S., L. E. Moser, and B. Anderson. 1986. "A Guide for Planning and Analyzing a Year-Round Forage Program." Nebraska Cooperative Extension Bulletin EC 86-113-C.

This book was written to provide general information on prairie ecology and ideas for potential management strategies for prairies. However, because every prairie has unique qualities based on its soil type, topography, average rainfall, management history, etc., and because the information provided in this book will be constantly updated, you should seek guidance from local experts who are familiar with the prairies in your area. The following is a sampling of agencies and organizations whose missions include providing assistance to people trying to manage prairies for biological diversity. This is not an exhaustive list and does not include for-profit companies, which can also be valuable sources of local information. Addresses are accurate as of January 2009.

National Organizations

These organizations have local offices throughout the country. You can find the office closest to you through their websites.

The Nature Conservancy
www.nature.org

U.S. Department of Agriculture
Natural Resources Conservation Service
www.nrcs.usda.gov

appendices

U.S. Fish and Wildlife Service
www.fws.gov

State Organizations
Every state has local agencies and organizations that can offer assistance to land-owners working with conservation projects.

ILLINOIS
Illinois Department of Natural Resources
www.dnr.state.il.us/orc/wildliferesources

INDIANA
Indiana Department of Natural Resources
www.state.in.us/dnr/fishwild/index2.htm

IOWA
Iowa Association of County Conservation Boards
www.iaccb.com

Iowa Department of Natural Resources
www.iowadnr.com/wildlife/index.html

Iowa Natural Heritage Foundation
www.inhf.org

Iowa Prairie Network
www.iowaprairienetwork.org

Tallgrass Prairie Center
www.tallgrassprairiecenter.org

KANSAS
Kansas Department of Wildlife and Parks
www.kdwp.state.ks.us

MINNESOTA

Minnesota Department of Natural Resources
www.dnr.state.mn.us

MISSOURI

Missouri Department of Conservation
www.conservation.state.mo.us

Missouri Prairie Foundation
www.moprairie.org

NEBRASKA

Nebraska Game and Parks Commission
www.ngpc.state.ne.us

Prairie Plains Resource Institute
www.prairieplains.org

NORTH DAKOTA

North Dakota Game and Fish Department
www.gf.nd.gov

OKLAHOMA

Oklahoma Department of Wildlife Conservation
www.wildlifedepartment.com

SOUTH DAKOTA

South Dakota Department of Game, Fish, and Parks
www.sdgfp.info/Wildlife/index.htm

WISCONSIN

The Prairie Enthusiasts
www.theprairieenthusiasts.org

Wisconsin Department of Natural Resources
www.dnr.state.wi.us

As you go looking for additional information on prairies and prairie management, this selection of resources may be helpful. The list includes field guides to identification of prairie species as well as references on prairie restoration and invasive species. This is not a comprehensive list, so check with local experts for other recommended reading.

Barkley, T. (ed). 1986. *Flora of the Great Plains*. Great Plains Flora Association. University Press of Kansas. A comprehensive list of plants from the Great Plains, along with descriptions and identification guides. Very technical, and not for everyone.

Curtis, J. T. 1959. *The Vegetation of Wisconsin*. University of Wisconsin Press. A classic book describing the composition and distribution of plant communities of Wisconsin, but an educational read for anyone in the central United States.

Czarapata, E. J. 2005. *Invasive Plants of the Upper Midwest*. University of Wisconsin Press. A guide to identifying invasive plants in multiple stages of growth and information about control methods.

Farrar, J. 1999. *Field Guide to Wildflowers of Nebraska and the Great Plains*. Nebraska Game and Parks Commission. An out-of-print but excellent field guide to western tallgrass and mixed-grass prairie plants.

Florasearch. Nebraska Statewide Arboretum. www.arboretum.unl.edu/florasearch. An online searchable database of common prairie plants. Useful for those unfamiliar with more technical guides and keys.

Haddock, M. J. 2005. *Wildflowers and Grasses of Kansas: A Field Guide*. University Press of Kansas. A great field guide for prairie plants in Kansas, also available online at www.kswildflower.org.

Iowa Prairie Network. www.iowaprairienetwork.org. A collection of information and announcements about prairie ecology, restoration, and news in Iowa.

Johnson, J. R., and G. E. Larson. 1999. *Grassland Plants of South Dakota and the Northern Great Plains*. College of Agriculture and Biological Sciences. South Dakota State University. An excellent field guide for northern mixed-grass prairie plants.

Kaufman, S. R., and W. Kaufman. 2007. *Invasive Plants: A Guide to Identification, Impacts, and Control of Common North American Species*. Stackpole Books.

Kaul, R. B., D. Sutherland, and S. Rolfsmeier. 2007. *The Flora of Nebraska*. School of Natural Resources, University of Nebraska–Lincoln. A comprehensive technical guide to identifying Nebraska plants. Useful distribution maps and descriptions of species, but may be a little daunting for amateurs.

Ladd, D. 2005. *Tallgrass Prairie Wildflowers*. Falcon Press. An excellent field guide for tallgrass prairie plants.

Packard, S., and C. F. Mutel. 1997. *The Tallgrass Prairie Restoration Handbook*. Society for Ecological Research. Island Press. Probably the most comprehensive book available on a wide range of prairie restoration techniques.

Prairie Nebraska. www.prairienebraska.org. A website for prairie enthusiasts in Nebraska and elsewhere. Information on prairie restoration and management and links to other sites.

Prairie Restoration: A Digital Aid Featuring Seeds, Seedlings, and Fruits. http://www.eiu.edu/%7Eprairie/index.htm.

Savage, C. 2004. *Prairie: A Natural History*. Greystone Books. An excellent nontechnical book about prairies for enthusiasts and potential enthusiasts.

Steinauer, G., W. Whitney, K. Adams, M. Bullerman, and C. Helzer. 2003. *A Guide to Prairie and Wetland Restoration in Eastern Nebraska*. Prairie Plains Resource Institute/Nebraska Game and Parks Commission. A practical no-nonsense guide to nontechnical but effective prairie restoration methods. Written for Nebraska prairies but applicable across the central United States.

Weaver, J. E. 1954. *North American Prairie*. Johnsen Publishing. A classic book on prairies by one of the first and best-known prairie ecologists.

Nomenclature follows the PLANTS Database: United States Department of Agriculture, Natural Resources Conservation, 2008. The PLANTS Database (http://plants.usda.gov, 18 July 2009). National Plant Data Center, Baton Rouge, LA 70874-4490, USA.

Annual sunflowers	*Helianthus annuus* L. and *H. petiolaris* Nutt.
Autumn olive	*Elaeagnus umbellata* Thunb.
Bermudagrass	*Cynodon dactylon* (L.) Pers.
Big bluestem	*Andropogon gerardii* Vitman.
Bird's-foot trefoil	*Lotus corniculatus* L.
Black cherry	*Prunus serotina* Ehrh.
Blackeyed Susan	*Rudbeckia hirta* L.
Black locust	*Robinia pseudoacacia* L.
Canada thistle	*Cirsium arvense* (L.) Scop.
Canada wildrye	*Elymus canadensis* L.
Caucasian (old world) bluestem	*Bothriochloa bladhii* (Retz.) S. T. Blake
Cheatgrass	*Bromus tectorum* L.
Common buckthorn	*Rhamnus cathartica* L.
Common (hairy) evening primrose	*Oenothera villosa* Thunb.
Cottonwood	*Populus deltoides* Bartram ex Marsh.
Crabgrass	*Digitaria* spp.

appendices

Creeping meadow foxtail	*Alopecurus arundinaceus* Poir.
Crownvetch	*Securigera varia* (L.) Lassen
Dames rocket	*Hesperis matronalis* L.
Dandelion	*Taraxacum officinale* F. H. Wigg.
Desert false indigo (false indigo)	*Amorpha fruticosa* L.
Eastern redcedar	*Juniperus virginiana* L. var. *virginian*
European (glossy) buckthorn	*Frangula alnus* Mill.
Foxtail barley	*Hordeum jubatum* L.
Green ash	*Fraxinus pennsylvanica* Marsh.
Hoary vervain	*Verbena stricta* Vent.
Honey locust	*Gleditsia triacanthos* L.
Honeysuckle species	*Lonicera* spp.
Indiangrass	*Sorghastrum nutans* (L.) Nash
Intermediate wheatgrass	*Thinopyrum intermedium* (Host) Barkworth & D. R. Dewey
Japanese (field) brome	*Bromus arvensis* L.
Johnsongrass	*Sorghum halepense* (L.) Pers.
Kentucky bluegrass	*Poa pratensis* L.
Leafy spurge	*Euphorbia esula* L.
Manystem pea	*Lathyrus polymorphus* Nutt.
Marbleseed (false gromwell)	*Onosmodium bejariense* DC. ex. A. DC. var. *occidentale* (Mack.) B. L. Turner
Maximilian sunflower	*Helianthus maximiliani* Schrad.
Musk (nodding plumeless) thistle	*Carduus nutans* L.
Osage orange	*Maclura pomifera* (Raf.) C. K. Schneid.
Oxalis	*Oxalis stricta* L.
Oxeye daisy	*Leucanthemum vulgare* Lam.
Persimmon	*Diospyros* sp.
Prairie cordgrass	*Spartina pectinata* Bosc ex Link
Prairie dropseed	*Sporobolus heterolepis* (A. Gray) A. Gray
Prairie fleabane	*Erigeron strigosus* Muhl. ex Willd.
Prairie ragwort (prairie groundsel)	*Packera plattensis* (Nutt.) W. A. Weber & A. Love
Purple loosestrife	*Lythrum salicaria* L.
Purple prairie clover	*Dalea purpurea* Vent.
Quackgrass	*Elymus repens* (L.) Gould
Ragweed	*Ambrosia* spp.

White mulberry	*Morus alba* L.
Redtop	*Agrostis gigantea* Roth
Reed canary grass	*Phalaris arundinacea* L.
Rough-leaved dogwood	*Cornus drummondii* C. A. Mey.
Russian olive	*Elaeagnus angustifolia* L.
Sandbar willow	*Salix interior* Rowlee
Sericea lespedeza	*Lespedeza cuneata* (Dum. Cours.) G. Don
Siberian elm	*Ulmus pumila* L.
Sixweeks fescue	*Vulpia octoflora* (Walter) Rydb.
Smooth brome	*Bromus inermis* Leyss.
Smooth sumac	*Rhus glabra* L.
Stiff goldenrod	*Oligoneuron rigidum* (L.) Small
Stiff sunflower	*Helianthus pauciflorus* Nutt.
Switchgrass	*Panicum virgatum* L.
Tall fescue	*Schedonorus phoenix* (Scop.) Holub.
Tall wheatgrass	*Thinopyrum ponticum* (Podp.) Z.-W. Liu & R.-C. Wang
Velvety gaura (velvetweed)	*Gaura mollis* James
Virginia wildrye	*Elymus virginicus* L.
Western wheatgrass	*Pascopyrum smithii* (Rydb.) A. Love
Wholeleaf rosinweed	*Silphium integrifolium* Michx.
Western ragweed (cuman ragweed)	*Ambrosia psilostachya* DC.
Wild indigo	*Baptisia bracteata* Muhl. ex Elliot
Witchgrass	*Panicum capillare* L.

Index

adaptive management, 69–78

big bluestem, 6, 7, 9, 10, 83, 85, 102, 109, 145
biodiversity. *See* biological diversity
biofuels, 174
biological diversity, 45, 67, 71, 78, 91, 103, 108, 113–114, 116, 118, 132, 143, 156–157, 171, 174, 205
biomass, 4, 26, 29, 91, 197
birds, 33–39, 45, 48, 59–62, 68, 94–95, 109, 122, 131, 137, 139–140, 171, 174, 197, 199; Bell's vireo, 139; bobolink, 34, 36, 59; bobwhite quail, 39, 122, 131, 139–140; brown-headed cowbird, 35; brown thrasher, 139, 140–141; dickcissel, 34, 36; grasshopper sparrow, 34–36, 59; grassland, 33–39, 48, 60–61, 68, 94–95, 137–139, 141, 150, 171, 174, 191, 197; greater prairie-chicken, 25, 33, 38–39, 52, 131; Henslow's sparrow, 34, 36, 74, 122, 138; loggerhead shrike, 139; meadowlarks, 34–36, 59; northern harrier, 48; orchard oriole, 139; ring-necked pheasant, 39, 44, 122, 139–140; sedge wren, 34, 36, 137; upland sandpiper, 34–35, 59, 122, 137
bison, 25, 27, 41, 42, 132; compared to cattle, 132–134; diet of, 20, 121; historical, 18, 162; present day, 19–20, 118. *See also* grazing

cattle. *See* grazing
Calendar Prairie Syndrome, 79
climate: change, 46, 173–175; historic, 1, 2, 14, 71, 171; and local ecotypes, 162; and patch-burn grazing, 130; and prairie type, 21, 26; and trees, 17, 130. *See also* weather

connectivity. *See* landscape ecology

cool-season exotic grasses. *See* invasive species

corridors. *See* landscape ecology

defoliation, 81–83, 85–86, 91, 94–95, 98–99, 104–106, 125, 149, 157, 195. *See also* grazing

disking, 96, 140, 164, 166, 185, 188

disturbance, 3, 10, 13, 20–21, 31, 44, 57, 81–82, 86, 88, 91, 96, 108, 114–115, 117, 131, 140, 159, 164, 169, 188

drought, 3, 7, 13, 21, 39, 57, 60, 68, 85–87, 100, 112, 144, 173, 182, 194. *See also* climate

edge effects. *See* landscape ecology

ethanol, 174

fire: and bison, 18–20; and climate, 21–23; and climate change, 175; and grazing, 117–122, 126–131, 137; and insects, 103, 105, 137; liability, 189; as management tool, 67, 71, 75–76, 81–82, 86–91, 99–105, 144–146, 148, 153, 164–166, 188, 194; as natural process, 1–3, 10, 13–18, 169, 171; planning, 184–187

global warming. *See* climate

grazing, 104–134, and birds, 36, 137; controlled random grazing, 115–117; and goats, 132, 157–159; and horses, 132; ice cream plants, 110–111; infrastructure for, 106, 181–182; leases, 157, 183; as management tool, 75, 86, 88–95, 104, 107, 144, 149, 151–155, 166, 194, 195; as natural process, 1–3, 10, 13, 17–20, 44, 47, 51, 57, 82–83, 88, 102, 105–106, 169; overgrazing,

36, 137; patch-burn grazing, 118–131; rotational grazing, 111–115; season-long single-pasture grazing, 108–111; and sheep, 132; stocking rate, 179–181. *See also* bison

habitat fragmentation, 29, 31, 38–41, 46, 48, 64, 71–72, 103, 112, 136–137, 140, 169, 171, 174

habitat patch. *See* landscape ecology

haying, 17, 36, 82, 86, 89–103, 132, 137, 141, 145, 194–195

herbicides, 2, 72, 91, 107, 144–158, 166, 169, 190–194; glyphosate, 156; triclopyr, 192

heterogeneity, 49–52, 54, 88, 95–96, 106, 109, 113, 114, 118, 122, 125, 131, 135, 137

insects, 2, 14, 18, 24–33, 38, 54, 56–57, 62, 95, 103–105, 109, 124, 135–137, 140; ants, 29–31, 64; beetles, 26–28; bugs, 27, 28, 31; butterflies, 27–28, 60, 64–65, 68, 136; decomposers, 33; dung beetles, 33; flies, 26, 28, 32–33; granivores, 27; grasshoppers, 18, 26, 29, 64, 105; herbivores, 18, 24, 26–27, 30; leafhoppers, 27, 103, 136; parasites, 32–33; parasitoids, 32–33; predators, 29–31; wasps, 26–28, 33. *See also* pollinators

interseeding, 140, 164, 166

invasive species, 10, 17, 56–57, 61–62, 64, 67–76, 81, 88–94, 96, 98–99, 107, 113, 115, 124, 126–132, 139–140, 143–159, 163, 171, 174–175, 183, 188, 190–195; autumn olive, 75–76, 149; bird's foot trefoil, 163; buckthorn, 149; Canada thistle, 72, 74, 75, 146, 155, 157; Caucasian bluestem, 144; cool-season exotic grasses, 89, 92, 94, 99, 102, 112,

Other Bur Oak Books of Interest

The Butterflies of Iowa
By Dennis W. Schlicht, John C. Downey, and Jeffrey Nekola

A Country So Full of Game: The Story of Wildlife in Iowa
By James J. Dinsmore

Deep Nature: Photographs from Iowa
Photographs by Linda Scarth and Robert Scarth, essay by John Pearson

The Elemental Prairie: Sixty Tallgrass Plants
By George Olson and John Madson

The Emerald Horizon: The History of Nature in Iowa
By Cornelia F. Mutel

Enchanted by Prairie
By Bill Witt and Osha Gray Davidson

An Illustrated Guide to Iowa Prairie Plants
By Paul Christiansen and Mark Müller

The Iowa Breeding Bird Atlas
By Laura Spess Jackson, Carol A. Thompson, and James J. Dinsmore

The Iowa Nature Calendar
By Jean C. Prior and James Sandrock,
   Illustrated by Claudia McGehee

Landforms of Iowa
By Jean C. Prior

A Practical Guide to
   Prairie Reconstruction
By Carl Kurtz

Prairie: A North American Guide
By Suzanne Winckler

Prairie in Your Pocket: A Guide to
   Plants of the Tallgrass Prairie
By Mark Müller

Prairies, Forests, and Wetlands:
   The Restoration of Natural
   Landscape Communities in Iowa
By Janette R. Thompson

Restoring the Tallgrass Prairie:
   An Illustrated Manual for Iowa
   and the Upper Midwest
By Shirley Shirley

A Tallgrass Prairie Alphabet
By Claudia McGehee

The Vascular Plants of Iowa:
   An Annotated Checklist
   and Natural History
By Lawrence J. Eilers and Dean M. Roosa

Where the Sky Began:
   Land of the Tallgrass Prairie
By John Madson

Wildflowers and Other Plants
   of Iowa Wetlands
By Sylvan T. Runkel and Dean M. Roosa

Wildflowers of Iowa Woodlands
By Sylvan T. Runkel and Alvin F. Bull

Wildflowers of the Tallgrass Prairie:
   The Upper Midwest
Sylvan T. Runkel and Dean M. Roosa

A Woodland Counting Book
By Claudia McGehee